NATURAL RESOURCES

NATURAL RESOURCES

Agriculture
Animals
Energy
Forests
Lands
Minerals
Plants
Water and Atmosphere

MINERALS

GIFTS FROM THE EARTH

Julie Kerr Casper, Ph.D.

CHELSEA HOUSE
PUBLISHERS

An imprint of Infobase Publishing

Minerals

Chelsea House
An imprint of Infobase Publishing
132 West 31st Street
New York NY 10001

Library of Congress Cataloging-in-Publication Data

Casper, Julie Kerr.
    Minerals : gifts from the Earth / Julie Kerr Casper.
        p. cm.—(Natural resources)
    Includes bibliographical references and index.
    ISBN-13: 978-0-8160-6357-4 (hardcover)
    ISBN-10: 0-8160-6357-5 (hardcover)
    1. Mines and mineral resources. 2. Minerals. I. Title. II. Series.

    TN146.C37 2007
    549—dc22   2006102275

Chelsea House books are available at special discounts when purchased in bulk quantities for businesses, associations, institutions, or sales promotions. Please call our Special Sales Department in New York at (212) 967-8800 or (800) 322-8755.

You can find Chelsea House on the World Wide Web at http://www.chelseahouse.com

Text design by Erik Lindstrom
Cover design by Ben Peterson

Printed in the United States of America

Bang NMSG 10 9 8 7 6 5 4 3 2 1

This book is printed on acid-free paper.

All links and Web addresses were checked and verified to be correct at the time of publication. Because of the dynamic nature of the Web, some addresses and links may have changed since publication and may no longer be valid.

CONTENTS

Mankind did not weave the web of life.
We are but one strand in it. Whatever we
do to the web, we do to ourselves . . .
All things are bound together.

—Chief Seattle

The Earth has been blessed with an abundant supply of natural resources. Natural resources are those elements that exist on the planet for the use and benefit of all living things. Scientists commonly divide them down into distinct groups for the purposes of studying them. These groups include agricultural resources, plants, animals, energy sources, landscapes, forests, minerals, and water and atmospheric resources.

One thing we humans have learned is that many of the important resources we have come to depend on are not renewable. *Nonrenewable* means that once a resource is depleted it is gone forever. The fossil fuel that gasoline is produced from is an example of a nonrenewable resource. There is only a finite supply, and once it is used up, that is the end of it.

While living things such as animals are typically considered renewable resources, meaning they can potentially be replenished, animals hunted to extinction become nonrenewable resources. As we know from past evidence, the extinctions of the dinosaurs, the woolly mammoth, and the saber-toothed tiger were complete. Sometimes, extinctions like this may be caused by natural factors, such as climate change, drought, or flood, but many extinctions are caused by the activities of humans.

Overhunting caused the extinction of the passenger pigeon, which was once plentiful throughout North America. The bald eagle was hunted to the brink of extinction before it became a protected species, and African elephants are currently threatened with extinction because they are still being hunted for their ivory tusks. Overhunting is only one potential threat, though. Humans are also responsible for habitat loss. When humans change land use and convert an animal's habitat to a city, this destroys the animal's living space and food sources and promotes its endangerment.

Plants can also be endangered or become extinct. An important issue facing us today is the destruction of the Earth's tropical rain forests. Scientists believe there may be medicinal value in many plant species that have not been discovered yet. Therefore, destroying a plant species could be destroying a medical benefit for the future.

Because of human impact and influence all around the Earth, it is important to understand our natural resources, protect them, use them wisely, and plan for future generations. The environment—land, soil, water, plants, minerals, and animals—is a marvelously complex and dynamic system that often changes in ways too subtle to perceive. Today, we have enlarged our vision of the landscape with which we interact. Farmers manage larger units of land, which makes their job more complex. People travel greater distances more frequently. Even when they stay at home, they experience and affect a larger share of the world through electronic communications and economic activities—and natural resources have made these advancements possible.

The pace of change in our society has accelerated as well. New technologies are always being developed. Many people no longer spend all their time focused in one place or using things in traditional ways. People now move from one place to another and are constantly developing and using new and different resources.

A sustainable society requires a sustainable environment. Because of this, we must think of natural resources in new ways. Today, more than ever, we must dedicate our efforts to conserve the land. We still live in a beautiful, largely natural world, but that world is quickly changing. World population growth and our desire to live comfortably are exerting pressures on our soil, air, water, and other natural resources. As we destroy and fragment natural habitats, we continue to push nonhuman life into ever-smaller pockets. Today, we run the risk of those places becoming isolated islands on a domesticated landscape.

In order to be responsible caretakers of the planet, it is important to realize that we humans have a partnership with the Earth and the other life that shares the planet with us. This series presents a refreshing and informative way to view the Earth's natural resources. *Agriculture: The Food We Grow and Animals We Raise* looks at agricultural resources to see how responsible conservation, such as caring for the soil, will give us continued food to feed growing populations. *Plants: Life From the Earth* examines the multitude of plants that exist and the role they play in biodiversity. The use of plants in medicines and in other products that people use every day is also covered.

In *Animals: Creatures That Roam the Planet,* the series focuses on the diverse species of animals that live on the planet, including the important roles they have played in the advancement of civilization. This book in the series also looks at habitat destruction, exotic species, animals that are considered in danger of extinction, and how people can help to keep the environment intact.

Next, in *Energy: Powering the Past, Present, and Future,* the series explores the Earth's energy resources—such as renewable power from water, ocean energy, solar energy, wind energy, and biofuels; and non-renewable sources from oil shale, tar sands, and fossil fuels. In addition, the future of energy and high-tech inventions on the horizon are also explored.

In *Lands: Taming the Wilds,* the series addresses the land and how civilizations have been able to tame deserts, mountains, arctic regions, forests, wetlands, and floodplains. The effects that our actions can have on the landscape for years to come are also explored. In *Forests: More Than Just Trees,* the series examines the Earth's forested areas and how unique and important these areas are to medicine, construction, recreation, and commercial products. The effects of deforestation, pest outbreaks, and wildfires—and how these can impact people for generations to come—are also addressed.

In *Minerals: Gifts From the Earth*, the bounty of minerals in the Earth and the discoveries scientists have made about them are examined. Moreover, this book in the series gives an overview of the critical part minerals play in many common activities and how they affect our lives every day.

Finally, in *Water and Atmosphere: The Lifeblood of Natural Systems*, the series looks at water and atmospheric resources to find out just how these resources are the lifeblood of the natural system—from drinking water, food production, and nutrient storage to recreational values. Drought, sea-level rise, soil management, coastal development, the effects of air and water pollution, and deep-sea exploration and what it holds for the future are also explored.

The reader will learn the wisdom of recycling, reducing, and reusing our natural resources, as well as discover many simple things that can be done to protect the environment. Practical approaches such as not leaving the water running while brushing your teeth, turning the lights off when leaving a room, using reusable cloth bags to transport groceries, building a backyard wildlife refuge, planting a tree, forming a carpool, or starting a local neighborhood recycling program are all explored.

Everybody is somebody's neighbor, and shared responsibility is the key to a healthy environment. The cheapest—and most effective—conservation comes from working with nature. This series presents things that people can do for the environment now and the important role we all can play for the future. As a wise Native-American saying goes, "We do not inherit the Earth from our ancestors—we borrow it from our children."

ACKNOWLEDGMENTS

Although we deal with different aspects of minerals every day, most people are not aware of just how much we depend on minerals as natural resources. We depend on them as a source of many services—some obvious, others not so obvious. Obvious uses are as building materials to construct our roads and homes with. Other, more subtle values, are in their aesthetic characteristics as art and jewelry; and the practical uses, such as for human health.

I hope to instill in you—the reader—an understanding and appreciation of minerals and their vital role in our environment. Perhaps by making you more aware of minerals and all that they do for each one of us every day, it will promote conservation of this precious resource and encourage environmental awareness and the desire to protect minerals and use them wisely on a long-term basis—a concept called resource stewardship.

I would sincerely like to thank the federal government agencies that study, manage, protect, and preserve our vast mineral resources—in particular, the U.S. Geological Survey (USGS), Bureau of Land Management (BLM), the U.S. Forest Service (USFS), the Natural Resources Conservation Service (NRCS), and the National Oceanic and Atmospheric Administration (NOAA) for providing an abundance of learning resources toward this important subject. I would also like to acknowledge the many universities across the country and their geology departments, as well as private organizations that diligently strive to protect our precious mineral resources, not only at home but also worldwide. Finally, I would also like to express appreciation to the Minerals Information Institute for the outstanding efforts they make to educate students about minerals and stewardship.

INTRODUCTION

The comfortable existence we enjoy today depends on the abundant use of mineral resources. Nearly everything we use is made from materials that have been extracted from the Earth. Minerals are important to our lives every day. Rocks contain the minerals that weather into soils and give vital nourishment to plants. Minerals provide us with many things essential to life. In fact, minerals touch our lives in hundreds of ways each day. Life as we know it would not exist without minerals. Anything that cannot be grown—that is neither plant nor animal—is a mineral or made from minerals and is obtained directly from the Earth.

Agriculture, construction, manufacturing, communication, transportation, electronics, art, and science—almost every area of human activity depends in some way on minerals. The raw materials we take out of the ground are as critical to our lifestyle as food and water are.

Humans use huge amounts of minerals each year, such as billions of tons of sand and gravel. In the United States alone, it takes more than 2 billion tons of minerals each year to maintain our standard of living—an equivalent to about 10 tons (9 metric tons) of minerals for every person. From those minerals come the products we need to live and those that make our lives comfortable.

Our dependence on minerals begins with one of the most basic requirements for life—food. Minerals are needed in many activities involved with providing what we eat. For example, fertilizers made from potash, phosphate rock, sulfur, and nitrogen help plants grow. Metal is used to make tractors and other farm equipment. Food processors use metal machines and equipment, and food is packaged in metal cans and other containers made from, or with, minerals.

People also need minerals to remain healthy. The foods we eat supply our bodies with essential minerals, such as iron, calcium, phosphorus, magnesium, copper, and zinc. Many people even take vitamins containing mineral supplements.

Minerals provide the building materials for houses, office buildings, roads, and bridges. Many of these products are extracted from pits, quarries, and other mines. Building materials, such as brick, stone, concrete, glass, tile, asphalt, gypsum wallboard, aluminum, iron, steel, metal appliances, furnaces, air conditioners, ventilation ducts, copper pipes, and electrical wiring are all made from mineral resources.

Many of the goods and products we use each day are made from minerals, such as stereos, televisions, DVD players, refrigerators, toasters, ovens, can openers, pots and pans, vacuums, doorknobs, curling irons, towel racks, irons, light fixtures, and lamps. The list of useful items just goes on—kitchen utensils, picture frames, bolts, screws, nails, plates, soaps and detergents made from boron, phosphates, toothpaste, aspirin tablets, lipstick, eye shadow, and other kinds of makeup all come originally from some form of mineral resource.

Many materials that are not in themselves minerals could not be manufactured without minerals. For example, minerals are involved in making glass, paper, and paints. Minerals actually make possible the manufacture of almost every product bought and sold today. For instance, the manufacturing processes involved in refining petroleum; making steel; and producing textiles, plastics, and fertilizers all depend on chemicals made from minerals.

Today, minerals are also critical for transportation. Cars, trucks, buses, trains, subways, barges, ships, and the cranes used to unload them are all made of metal. Cars, for example, contain iron and steel, manganese, chromium, platinum, zinc, lead, copper, and aluminum. Streets, highways, and bridges are made from asphalt, sand, gravel, and concrete. In the winter, road crews use sand and salt to keep traffic from skidding on snow and ice. Even the gas that is used to operate cars and other methods of transportation was manufactured by using mineral-based chemicals.

Airplanes, satellites, missiles, and spacecraft are also made from minerals and metals. They depend on the permanence, strength, durability, reliability, and corrosion resistance of the metals used to make them.

Advances in electronics and computer technology depend on minerals. Copper is able to conduct electricity, and, because of this, it has made possible the development of many electronic items. Directly, or indirectly, the electronics and computer industries use almost every mineral that is mined commercially today. For instance, according to the U.S. Geological Survey, it takes 42 different minerals to make a telephone handset.

Minerals also provide artists with the important materials they need, such as pigments for color, clay, and marble. A photographer relies on the silver that is used in the manufacture of film. Many musical instruments are made from metal, as well as much of the equipment used in science, such as microscopes, supercomputers, test tubes, and other highly sophisticated and specialized equipment.

The extraction, processing, and transport of minerals, however, inevitably have impacts on the environment. Monitoring and controlling disruption of landscapes and ecosystems—while ensuring supplies of critical minerals—is a technological challenge.

This volume in the Natural Resources series takes an in-depth look at the minerals, metals, and elements that people depend heavily on each day. Chapter 1 looks at mineral resources, elements, metals, and compounds—how they form, where they occur, and the far-reaching implications they have for our economy and survival. Chapter 2 examines the history of minerals and their impact on the development of civilization—the Stone Age, the Bronze Age, Iron Age, the Industrial Revolution, and the world's most famous gold rushes. Chapter 3 explores different types of mineral resources, both renewable and nonrenewable, and the properties that make them valuable to humans and ecosystems. Chapter 4 deals with the development of various mineral resources and the mining techniques involved in order to extract, process, and refine the various commodities into useful resources.

Chapter 5 examines the various uses and impacts of minerals in industry, agriculture, science, technology, medical applications, and a host of other applications.

Chapter 6 outlines the importance of minerals and the multitude of goods and services they provide that contribute to the quality of our lives every day. Chapter 7 explores various management issues associated with the management of mineral resources, such as the effects of minerals on water, soil, plants, and the atmosphere; reclamation of mining operations and its connection to a healthy environment; natural and recycled resources; and hazardous waste management. Chapter 8 looks at the importance of conservation of mineral resources; the critical role of recycling, reducing, and reusing mineral resources; appropriate substitutes to mineral resources; and the development of new technology and its potential applications to effective conservation. Finally, Chapter 9 focuses on the future issues of mineral resources; environmental issues of current mining practices; future mining and search methodologies; undiscovered mineral resources; minerals in the ocean and why they represent a new frontier for minerals; and manganese nodules, and other underwater treasures and the impact they can have on our future.

CONCEPTS OF MINERAL RESOURCES

Mineral resources are found on and within the Earth's crust. More than 3,500 different minerals have already been identified. Minerals are everywhere around us. For instance, it is estimated that more than 70 million tons (63.5 million metric tons) of gold is contained in the oceans alone. Much of this is too expensive to be recovered, however, because it is scattered over wide areas. In order for it to be economical to recover (mine), minerals must be sufficiently concentrated into deposits by the Earth's natural processes.

There are three classes of mineral resources—metals, **nonmetals**, and fuels. Gold, silver, iron, nickel, and copper are examples of metallic mineral resources. Common minerals—such as sand, gravel, limestone, salt, and clay—are examples of nonmetallic mineral resources. These nonmetallic minerals are also referred to as industrial minerals. Minerals used as a fuel source include oil, gas, and coal and are referred to as **fossil fuels.** Uranium, used for the production of nuclear energy, is a metallic fuel.

This chapter examines the various mineral resources; what **elements** and **compounds** are and their importance to the periodic table; properties of minerals, metals, and gemstones; the **rock cycle** and its role toward determining where various mineral resources are found; and finally, minerals and materials in the twenty-first century.

MINERAL RESOURCES

Minerals are much more than beautiful display pieces—they are the basic building blocks of the universe. Minerals make up the Earth, the Moon, and the meteorites that travel through the vast expanses of space. Mineral resources are the natural minerals obtained from the Earth by humans. Resources are those substances that people use directly, or make products out of, to add value, convenience, and quality to their lives. Minerals contain information that allows scientists to explore and learn about the world. Modern civilization relies heavily on mineral resources. In fact, if a commodity is not derived from a plant or animal, then it probably came from a **rock** or mineral.

Objects made from mineral resources are everywhere; some are obvious, others are not so obvious. **Metal** objects, stone for retaining walls, and sand for playgrounds and baseball fields are obvious uses of minerals. Items like toothpaste, chalk, cups, glass, and computer circuitry are also derived from minerals, although not obviously so. In addition, plastics and many of the fibers from which cloth is made come from coal or oil—also mineral resources found in the Earth.

Geology plays a critical role in the formation and location of mineral resources. By examining different kinds of rock formations and by studying the Earth's surface, geologists can interpret the geologic environments in which mineral resources may be found. For a long time, people were able to find enough mineral resources on the surface of the Earth. This, however, is not the case with many mineral resources today. Once a vein of silver or a bed of coal has been mined, it cannot be replaced—it is a nonrenewable resource.

Minerals in the past have been discovered through various prospecting methods. Some mineral deposits are exposed on hillsides where **overburden** (the rock lying on top of the deposits) has been exposed. When looking for mineral resources, such as gold, many prospectors have panned in rivers. Prospectors over the previous centuries often went out with a mule to carry mining equipment—such as shovels and picks—and hunted for minerals using trial, error, and sometimes luck.

What Makes That Lightbulb Work?

The next time you turn on a simple lightbulb so that you can see better indoors, think about what mineral resources went into it in order to make it work.

- Soft glass is made from silica, trona (soda ash), lime, coal, and salt. Hard glass is made from the same minerals and is used for some lamps to withstand higher temperatures.
- The filament is made of tungsten.
- The lead-in-wires are made of copper and nickel and are used to carry the current to and from the filament.
- The tie wires are made from molybdenum.
- The fuse (which protects the lamp and circuit if the filament arcs) is made of nickel, manganese, copper and/or silicon alloys.
- The heat deflector is made of aluminum. This is necessary to reduce the movement of hot gases into the neck of the bulb.
- The base is made of brass (copper and zinc) or aluminum.
- Molybdenum wires support the filament.
- The gas in the bulb is usually a mixture of nitrogen and argon.
- For the generation of electricity, fuel resources such as coal, nuclear, hydropower, natural gas, or oil are used.

Without minerals, none of this would be possible.

Source: Mineral Information Institute

Because the majority of surface minerals have already been discovered and used, geologists today use a variety of specialized tools and instruments to help locate mineral resources. Geologists have to work through hundreds to thousands of feet of overburden using every geologic, hydrochemical, geochemical, and geophysical method available to assist in the search. All mineral resources—even sand and gravel—require some form of concentration process to make mining a mineral deposit economically feasible because the natural abundance of the sought-after element in the Earth's crust is normally too low to be a commercial deposit.

Geologists use airplanes and helicopters with photographic equipment. They also use magnetic- and gravity-detecting equipment, which gives information about the Earth's subsurface. Geologists sometimes use pictures taken from satellites in their search for hidden mineral resources. Fortunately, most of the mineral commodities—including uranium—go through a concentration process that provides a much broader target for exploration than the mineral deposit itself. These processes leave evidence of their presence over an area a few times to a few hundred times the size of the mineral deposits themselves. This allows the prospecting team to locate the actual **mineralization** much more efficiently in terms of both time and money.

The value of the wealth in rocks has long been understood. Countries eager to gain more of the Earth's riches for themselves have fought wars over minerals. In addition, hundreds of thousands of prospectors have rushed to places where diamonds, gold, silver, and other precious metals and minerals have been discovered.

There are hundreds of mineral resources in the Earth. The table on page 5 lists some of the most prevalent minerals and what they are used for, which will be discussed in more detail in later chapters.

Minerals affect all aspects of our lives, and without knowing it most people use a tremendous amount of mineral resources every day, all year long. The figure on page 6 shows the yearly per capita consumption of new minerals that is necessary to maintain present-day standards of living.

Minerals and Their Uses

Mineral	Use
Aluminum	Aluminum cans and other lightweight products
Asbestos	Construction material, insulation, fire retardant, soundproofing material, floor covering, ceiling tiles, roofing materials, pipe, sheeting
Asphalt	Road-paving material
Basalt	Aggregate, road ballast, road material
Bismuth	Pharmaceuticals, chemicals, ceramics, paints, catalysts
Brines	Salts
Cement	Construction material
Clay	Paper coaters and fillers, ceramic products, rubber fillers, bricks, decorative tile
Coal	Heat, energy
Copper	Refined copper, copper sulfate, copper products
Fluorspar	Used in manufacture of steel, aluminum, glass, and fluorocarbons
Galena	Used in automobiles, electronics, radiation protection
Gemstones	Jewelry, decorative art
Gold	Jewelry, decorative art, electronics
Graphite	Lead pencils, paints, as a lubricant and an electrode, and in nuclear reactors
Gypsum	Wallboard, cement, used to make plaster of Paris
Iron	Construction of steel products
Mercury	Used in dental fillings, thermometers, switches, thermostats, fluorescent light bulbs and tubes
Molybdenum	Alloy for jet engines, automotive parts, high-speed drills, offshore piping, lubricants, and catalysts
Potash	Forestry fertilization, feed supplement, recycling flux in aluminum industry
Sand	Used as an abrasive, in a foundry, and to make glass and pottery
Talc	Filler in roofing materials, paper, plastic, synthetic rubber, and ceramic materials
Titanium	High-strength alloy in aircraft and shipbuilding

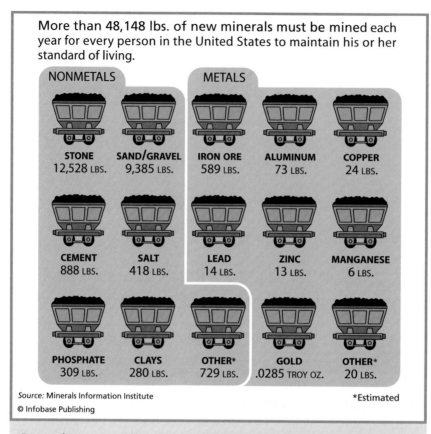

More than 48,148 lbs. of new minerals must be mined each year for every person in the United States to maintain his or her standard of living.

NONMETALS

METALS

STONE	SAND/GRAVEL	IRON ORE	ALUMINUM	COPPER
12,528 LBS.	9,385 LBS.	589 LBS.	73 LBS.	24 LBS.

CEMENT	SALT	LEAD	ZINC	MANGANESE
888 LBS.	418 LBS.	14 LBS.	13 LBS.	6 LBS.

PHOSPHATE	CLAYS	OTHER*	GOLD	OTHER*
309 LBS.	280 LBS.	729 LBS.	.0285 TROY OZ.	20 LBS.

Source: Minerals Information Institute   *Estimated
© Infobase Publishing

Per capita consumption of raw minerals. Every year, more than 48,000 pounds (21,772 kilograms) of new minerals must be provided for every person in the United States in order to maintain the standard of living we enjoy today.

ELEMENTS, COMPOUNDS, AND THE PERIODIC TABLE

Some minerals occur uncombined with other minerals (called native elements), but they are usually combined with other materials. It usually takes great effort to obtain riches from the Earth. It took thousands of years of trial and error, of experimentation with rocks and minerals, to discover the various uses of minerals. Oftentimes, minerals are initially overlooked because they are locked up as chemical compounds and need to be processed in some special way in order to make them useful resources. Therefore, in order to understand minerals and the role they play in rock and certain geologic formations, it is necessary to understand the building blocks that made them. These building blocks are elements and compounds.

Elements are the simple building blocks of the Earth. Minerals are made up of one or more elements. All substances are made of elements and compounds, or a **mixture** of the two. The science of chemistry is the study of elements and compounds. Experiments have allowed scientists to discover about 113 elements so far. They have also learned how these elements combine to make compounds and have even discovered and made new ones.

An element is a substance made up of just one type of atom. For example, oxygen is an element because it contains only oxygen atoms. An element is the simplest type of substance there is. A compound is a substance composed of different elements joined together. Water is a compound because it is made up of the elements oxygen and hydrogen (H_2O). The atoms of the elements are connected by chemical bonds. By combining different elements together, it is possible to build millions of different compounds.

A mixture is a substance that contains different elements and compounds—but these are not joined together by chemical bonds. This means that a mixture can always be separated into the individual substances that it contains. For example, the air we breathe is a mixture, because it is composed of oxygen, nitrogen, and carbon dioxide.

In the field of chemistry, every known element has a name and a chemical symbol assigned to it. The symbol is an abbreviation of the element's name and scientists use these symbols to represent the elements in chemical formulas and equations. For example, the chemical symbol for the element hydrogen is H; for oxygen it is O. The symbol does not always match the element's name, however. For example, the symbol for iron is Fe—not I. This is because the symbols can come from different languages. In the case of the element iron, the symbol Fe stands for *ferrum*—the Latin word for iron. If the element only has a one-letter identifier, it is shown as an uppercase letter; if it has two, it is shown as an uppercase letter followed by a lowercase letter. Each element's symbol is denoted in the periodic table, as shown on page 9.

The periodic table is a list of all of Earth's known elements. In the table, the elements are arranged so that elements with similar properties are close together. In fact, the periodic table gets its name from the fact that the elements' properties repeat themselves every few elements—or *periodically*. Because of the way the table is ordered, a chemist can tell what the properties of an element are likely to be just by looking at its position in the table.

The vertical columns of elements are called **groups**. The horizontal rows of elements are called **periods**. The table also often uses colors to show which elements are metals (blue in the table on page 9), which are nonmetals (yellow), and which are metalloids (pink).

The two main classes in the periodic table are the metals and non-metals. Roughly 75% of the elements are metals and are located on the left side of the table. The nonmetals are located on the right side.

All metals appear shiny. Some metals lose their shine when they react with oxygen in the air—such as copper, which turns a greenish tint after long-term exposure to the atmosphere. Polishing the metal can restore the shine. Most metals are hard, and they are also **malleable**, which means that they can be bent into different shapes without breaking. They are also **ductile**, meaning they can be pulled thinner and longer without breaking. All metals—except mercury—are solids at room temperature, because metals usually have high melting points and high boiling points. For instance, iron melts at 2,795°F (1,535°C), and boils at 5,182°F (2,861°C).

All metals let heat and electricity pass through them easily, which makes them good conductors of heat and electricity. Because metals, like copper, are such good conductors of electricity, they are commonly used in wiring. Only a few metals, such as iron, are magnetic.

All metals share similar properties. Nonmetals, however, have a wide range of different properties. At room temperature, most nonmetals

PERIODIC TABLE OF THE ELEMENTS

Key:
- Atomic number
- Symbol — Li
- Atomic weight — 6.941 (atomic number 3)

1 IA	2 IIA	3 IIIB	4 IVB	5 VB	6 VIB	7 VIIB	8 VIIIB	9 VIIIB	10 VIIIB	11 IB	12 IIB	13 IIIA	14 IVA	15 VA	16 VIA	17 VIIA	18 VIIIA
1 H 1.00794																	2 He 4.0026
3 Li 6.941	4 Be 9.0122											5 B 10.81	6 C 12.011	7 N 14.0067	8 O 15.9994	9 F 18.9984	10 Ne 20.1798
11 Na 22.9898	12 Mg 24.3051											13 Al 26.9815	14 Si 28.0855	15 P 30.9738	16 S 32.067	17 Cl 35.4528	18 Ar 39.948
19 K 39.0938	20 Ca 40.078	21 Sc 44.9559	22 Ti 47.867	23 V 50.9415	24 Cr 51.9962	25 Mn 54.938	26 Fe 55.845	27 Co 58.9332	28 Ni 58.6934	29 Cu 63.546	30 Zn 65.409	31 Ga 69.723	32 Ge 72.61	33 As 74.9216	34 Se 78.96	35 Br 79.904	36 Kr 83.798
37 Rb 85.4678	38 Sr 87.62	39 Y 88.906	40 Zr 91.224	41 Nb 92.9064	42 Mo 95.94	43 Tc (98)	44 Ru 101.07	45 Rh 102.9055	46 Pd 106.42	47 Ag 107.8682	48 Cd 112.412	49 In 114.818	50 Sn 118.711	51 Sb 121.760	52 Te 127.60	53 I 126.9045	54 Xe 131.29
55 Cs 132.9054	56 Ba 137.328	57–70 ☆	72 Hf 178.49	73 Ta 180.948	74 W 183.84	75 Re 186.207	76 Os 190.23	77 Ir 192.217	78 Pt 195.08	79 Au 196.9655	80 Hg 200.59	81 Tl 204.3833	82 Pb 207.2	83 Bi 208.9804	84 Po (209)	85 At (210)	86 Rn (222)
87 Fr (223)	88 Ra (226)	89–102 ★	104 Rf (261)	105 Db (262)	106 Sg (266)	107 Bh (262)	108 Hs (263)	109 Mt (268)	110 Ds (271)	111 Rg (272)	112 Uub (277)						

☆ Lanthanoids

57 La 138.9055	58 Ce 140.115	59 Pr 140.908	60 Nd 144.24	61 Pm (145)	62 Sm 150.36	63 Eu 151.966	64 Gd 157.25	65 Tb 158.9253	66 Dy 162.500	67 Ho 164.9303	68 Er 167.26	69 Tm 168.9342	70 Yb 173.04	71 Lu 174.967

★ Actinoids

89 Ac (227)	90 Th 232.0381	91 Pa 231.036	92 U 238.0289	93 Np (237)	94 Pu (244)	95 Am 243	96 Cm (247)	97 Bk (247)	98 Cf (251)	99 Es (252)	100 Fm (257)	101 Md (258)	102 No (259)	103 Lr (260)

Numbers in parentheses are atomic mass numbers of most stable isotopes.

© Infobase Publishing

The periodic table is a chart of all the known elements. The elements are arranged in order of their atomic numbers, but in rows, so that elements with similar properties are underneath each other. Each block in the table contains information including the element's name, chemical symbol, atomic number, and atomic mass. It also designates which elements are metals (blue), nonmetals (yellow), and metalloids (pink). The position of an element in the periodic table gives an idea of what its properties are likely to be.

are gases, but some are solid, and one—bromine—is a liquid. Nonmetals do not have consistent properties because they have a wide range of melting and boiling points.

Nonmetals (with the exception of carbon) are not good conductors of electricity or heat. In addition, all nonmetals are nonmagnetic. The table on page 16 illustrates the properties of metals and nonmetals.

Elements that have properties of both metals and nonmetals are called **metalloids**, or semimetals. Metalloids are very valuable in the manufacture of **semiconductors**. A semiconductor is a material that can conduct some electricity better than an insulator (a poor conductor of electricity) can, but not as much or as well as a metal can. Semiconductors are mainly used in electronic components and microchips in the computer industry.

Some metals react well with common chemicals, such as air, water, and **acids**. Others do not react at all. The **reactivity series** represents some common metals in order of how **reactive** they are, or how well they react with other chemicals.

Metals at the top of the series (potassium, sodium) are extremely reactive and are located in Group 1 of the periodic table. They react quickly with air to form metal oxides and so they must be kept away from air; they are stored in oil. When highly reactive metals are put in acid, chemical reactions occur, which produce hydrogen gas and excessive heat. The heat ignites the hydrogen and makes it explode. The

Groups of the Periodic Table

Group number	Group type
1	The alkali metals
2	The alkaline earth metals
17	The halogens
18	The noble gases

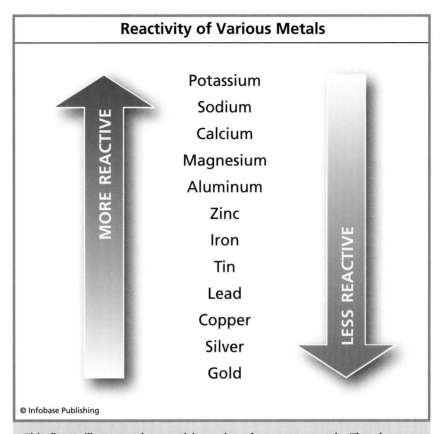

Reactivity of Various Metals

Potassium
Sodium
Calcium
Magnesium
Aluminum
Zinc
Iron
Tin
Lead
Copper
Silver
Gold

MORE REACTIVE

LESS REACTIVE

© Infobase Publishing

This figure illustrates the reactivity series of common metals. The elements at the top are the most reactive with other chemicals, such as acids, air, and water. Potassium and sodium are extremely reactive. They are found in Group 1 of the periodic table and react quickly with the air to make metal oxides. The metals at the bottom, such as gold and silver, are not reactive at all. They do not even react with strong acids such as hydrochloric acid.

metals at the bottom of the reactivity series—such as gold and silver— are not reactive, even with strong acids. The natural characteristics of these metals allow them to be used for specific resources.

Most of the elements in the periodic table occur naturally. They are found all over, such as in rocks, water, air, plants, and animals. Abundant elements—such as carbon and oxygen—are found in large quantities all around the Earth, but other elements only occur in tiny amounts in limited locations, which affects their value as natural resources. In addition, some elements occur naturally with others as a mixture. For example, pure gold is found in the ground. Most elements, however, are found in compounds.

Dmitri Mendeleyev

Dmitri Mendeleyev was a Russian scientist who first realized that if all the known elements were arranged in a table—by **atomic weight**—elements with similar properties and characteristics would group together. Elements that lie next to one another in the table would share certain qualities. He began by first writing all the elements and their atomic weights onto a series of index cards. Next, he tried to arrange the index cards in different patterns in order to determine the best "fit." He eventually ended up with an arrangement that he was satisfied with, in which elements with similar properties were grouped in vertical columns. Developed in 1869, this became known as the periodic table.

One of the most amazing things about Mendeleyev's table was that it had blank areas in which a particular substance should theoretically exist. He realized that the gaps were not errors but instead represented elements that had not yet been discovered. Because of the way he arranged his table, scientists were able to figure out what characteristics these theoretical elements should have. Later, as more and more elements were discovered, they did indeed have the properties Mendeleyev predicted they would, adding further credence to his table.

Mendeleyev's table was highly reliable. In the places where he had difficulty in placing an element, it turned out that what was previously believed about the element was wrong. Then, when more accurate information became available, the elements in question fit perfectly.

Mendeleyev's initial periodic table has, however, been modified over the years as scientists have gained more knowledge of the elements. Even still, his work represents one of the greatest advances to science and has proved to be a crucial tool.

Chemicals combine to release the energy necessary for liftoff of the space shuttle. *(Courtesy of NASA)*

Humans use nearly all the elements for various applications, such as in industry, agriculture, manufacturing, science, and medicine. Before elements can be useful as resources, they must be extracted (dug up) from where they are found. Different chemical and physical processes are used to extract the elements.

Metals—highly useful resources—are extracted from rocks in the Earth's crust. Rocks contain minerals called ores. An **ore** is a compound made up of a metal combined with other elements. People use many

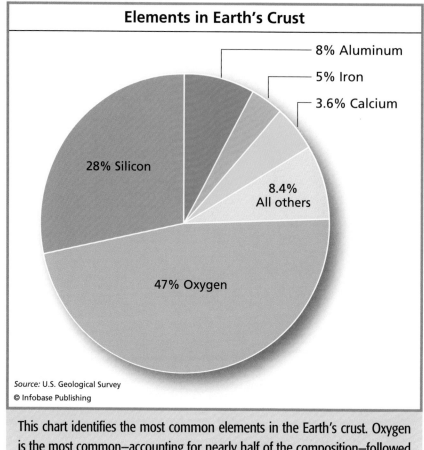

Elements in Earth's Crust

8% Aluminum

5% Iron

3.6% Calcium

28% Silicon

8.4% All others

47% Oxygen

Source: U.S. Geological Survey
© Infobase Publishing

This chart identifies the most common elements in the Earth's crust. Oxygen is the most common—accounting for nearly half of the composition—followed by silicon.

metals that are easy to extract (separate) from ores to be used for construction, industry, and many other applications. Metals are often mixed with each other—or even with nonmetals—to produce **alloys**. Alloys have more useful properties than the metals they are made from, such as increased strength.

Common metals include iron, copper, and aluminum. Iron is one of the most widely used metals. Most iron is used in the production of steel—steel is an alloy containing about 99% iron and 1% carbon. Steel

Because of its strength and durability, steel (an alloy of iron and carbon) is critical in the construction of high-rise buildings. *(Courtesy of Nature's Images)*

is used extensively in the construction of buildings, cars, ships, bridges, and many other useful objects that require great strength.

Because copper is such an easy metal to shape and cut and is also a good conductor of electricity, it is used extensively to make wires, cables, and pipes for water and heating systems. When copper is combined with zinc, it makes a stronger alloy called brass. Aluminum is another highly useful metal. Because of its low **density**, it is used to produce soft-drink cans, pots, pans, and aluminum foil—everyday products we cannot live without.

Most metals are in the center of the periodic table, in Groups 3 through 12. They are hard, strong metals with high melting and boiling points and high densities. The most commonly used transition metals are copper, zinc, iron, gold, and silver. Transition metals can be mixed with iron, steel, or aluminum to make various alloys for engineering. Some, such as palladium and platinum, are used in factories as catalysts to speed up chemical reactions.

Common nonmetals include carbon, hydrogen, phosphorus, nitrogen, oxygen, sulfur, the noble gases, and the halogens. One unique nonmetal is carbon. It occurs in two very different forms—diamond and graphite. Graphite is what pencil leads are made from, and it is the only nonmetal substance that conducts electricity. Diamond is used not only in jewelry, but also for the blades of cutting tools because

Properties of Metals and Nonmetals

Metals	Nonmetals
Less abundant in nature	More abundant in nature
Share similar properties	Have different properties
Mostly solids at room temperature	Mostly gases at room temperature
Oxides are basic	Oxides are acidic
Hard, shiny, and malleable	Weak, dull, and brittle
High densities	Low densities
High boiling and melting points	Low boiling and melting points
Good conductors of heat	Poor conductors of heat
Good conductors of electricity	Poor conductors of electricity

of its extreme hardness. Although they are both carbon, the difference between graphite and diamond is due to the atoms being joined together in different ways.

Hydrogen is the simplest of all elements (it is the first one listed in the periodic table). At room temperature, it is a colorless, odorless gas that is extremely flammable. Hydrogen is used to produce chemicals and fertilizer. It is extracted from natural gas.

Phosphorus is a solid that occurs in white and red forms. Red phosphorus is used to make matches and distress flares. White phosphorus is poisonous. It can be used to fill grenades. Nitrogen is a colorless, odorless gas, which composes 78% of the air in the atmosphere. Nitrogen is vital for the health of plants. In industry, it is used to create ammonia and nitric acid, which can be used to manufacture fertilizers and explosives. Oxygen is also a colorless, odorless gas that makes up 21% of the air we breathe. It is the most common element in the rocks of the Earth's crust.

Sulfur is a yellow solid, commonly found in areas of volcanic activity. Yellowstone National Park has a good display of sulfuric hot pots. Sulfur has many uses; it is used in the manufacture of sulfuric acid, and as an additive to the rubber in tires to extend the life of the rubber. The noble gases are all unreactive. This means that they almost never react with other elements to make compounds. They are commonly used in the bulbs of illuminated advertising signs.

The halogens—elements in Group 17—include fluorine, chlorine, and iodine. Fluorine is used in the production of nonstick coatings, chlorine is used as a disinfectant (such as commonly used in swimming pools), iodine is used in people's diets and also as an antiseptic (to sterilize cuts). In addition, many types of light bulbs—such as those in car headlights—are filled with halogen gases.

MINERALOGY AND MINERALS

Mineralogy is the branch of geology that deals with the classification and properties of minerals. It is closely related to petrology, the branch of geology that deals with the occurrence, origin, and history of rocks. As we have seen, minerals are the basic building blocks of rocks, soil, and sand. Most minerals (like quartz or mica) are abundant and common. Others, such as diamonds, rubies, sapphires, gold, and silver, are rare and very valuable. An important attribute of minerals is that they contain information about the chemical and physical conditions in the region of the Earth where they formed. Specific conditions must exist for a mineral to form. Minerals can help geologists determine which tectonic environment a given rock was created in. They can also relate information about the inaccessible portions of the Earth. National economies can be based on exploitation of mineral wealth; for instance, South Africa is a rich nation because of its abundant gold and diamond mineral resources.

The two most important characteristics of minerals are their composition and structure. The composition of minerals describes the kinds of chemical elements present and their proportions, whereas the structure of minerals describes the way in which the atoms of the chemical elements are packed together.

There are more than 3,500 known minerals, most made out of the eight most common mineral-forming elements. These eight elements

Common Mineral-forming Elements

Element	Symbol	Percentage of continental crust mass
Oxygen	O	46.6
Silicon	Si	27.7
Aluminum	Al	8.1
Iron	Fe	5.0
Calcium	Ca	3.6
Sodium	Na	2.8
Potassium	K	2.6
Magnesium	Mg	2.1

Source: U.S. Geological Survey

make up more than 98% of the mass of the continental crust. The eight most common mineral-forming elements are listed in the table on page 18.

The Properties of Minerals

Minerals have specific properties determined by their chemistry and **crystal** structure. Certain properties are characteristic of certain minerals and are used to identify them. The most common properties are crystal form, color, hardness, **streak, luster, cleavage, fracture,** transparency, and taste.

When a mineral forms freely, it forms a characteristic geometric solid bounded by geometrically arranged plane surfaces (which is the crystal form). This symmetry is an external expression of the symmetric internal arrangement of atoms, such as in repeating tetrahedron arrays. Individual crystals of the same mineral may look somewhat different because the relative sizes of individual faces may vary, but the angle between faces is constant and diagnostic for each mineral.

Every mineral has a characteristic crystal form. Some minerals have such distinctive forms that they can be readily identified without measuring angles between crystal faces. Examples of crystal form include cubic, rhombic, hexagonal, and tetragonal. **Pyrite** is recognized as interlocking growths of cubes; asbestos forms long, silky fibers. These distinctive characteristics are known as *growth habit*. The habit is the characteristic appearance of a crystal. Several descriptive terms to identify a crystal's habit are as follows: (1) prismatic, (2) acicular (slender, needlelike masses), (3) dendritic (having a plantlike shape), (4) bladed (looks like the blade of a knife), (5) prismatic (made out of prisms), (6) reniform (rounded kidney-shaped masses), and (7) massive (no definitive shape). Minerals are also described in terms of their **twinning**. Twinning refers to a nonparallel, symmetrical intergrowth of two or more crystals of the same species. Twinning can occur by contact and growth and can appear as a radiating mass of touching contact crystals or crystals that actually join and grow together.

Cleavage is the tendency of a mineral to break in preferred directions along bright, reflective planar surfaces. It results from the way in which the molecules of a mineral pack together. Cleavage occurs along planes where the bonds between the atoms are relatively weak.

Luster is the quality and intensity of light reflected from a mineral. It results from the way in which light is reflected from the molecules of a mineral. Typical lusters include metallic (like a polished metal), **vitreous** (like a polished glass), resinous (like resin), pearly (like a pearl), and greasy (oily).

Color results from the wavelengths of light that are reflected from the molecules of a mineral. Color is not reliable for identification of minerals, however, since it is commonly determined by elements that are not primary to the chemical composition of the mineral. This phenomenon is known as ionic substitution. For example, sapphires and rubies are both varieties of the mineral corundum (aluminum oxide), but are different colors due to different ionic substitutions. The color of the streak that a mineral leaves on a porcelain plate, however, can be used to identify **opaque** minerals with metallic lusters.

The density of a mineral is a measure of mass per unit volume. In other words, density describes how heavy a mineral feels. Specific gravity is an indirect measure of density; it is the ratio of the weight of a substance to the weight of an equal volume of water.

Streak is the color of a mineral's powder when rubbing it across the surface of an unglazed porcelain tile. Streak is a better diagnostic than color, because it is more consistent.

Hardness is a measure of the mineral's relative resistance to scratching. It results from the cohesion of the molecules in a mineral. Hardness is governed by the strength of bonds between atoms and is very distinctive and useful for mineral identification. A mineral's hardness can be determined by the ease with which one mineral can scratch another. For instance, talc (used for talcum powder) is the softest mineral, whereas diamond is the hardest mineral. Hardness is commonly measured using Mohs' scale (see table on page 22).

These quartz crystals exhibit twinning, a symmetrical intergrowth of two or more crystals of the same type. *(Courtesy of Nature's Images)*

Fracture is another way to identify minerals. If a mineral is struck with a geologic hammer and it breaks, leaving surfaces that are rough and uneven, it is said to fracture. While cleavage surfaces are usually flat and will produce exactly the same shape by repeated hammer blows, this is not the case with fracture. Most minerals fracture and cleave, but some will only fracture, such as quartz.

Transparency, another indicator used in mineral identification, refers to the way in which light passes through a mineral. It depends on the way mineral atoms are bonded. Mineral specimens through which objects can be seen are called **transparent**. If light passes through, but the object cannot be clearly seen, then the specimen is **translucent**. When light does not pass through a specimen, even when cut very thin, it is **opaque**. All these distinct properties enable a **mineralogist** to correctly identify the mineral being classified.

Gemstones

A natural gemstone is a mineral or stone, or organic matter that can be cut and polished for use as jewelry or another ornament. A precious gemstone has beauty, durability (resistance to abrasion, fracturing, and chemical reactions), and rarity, whereas a semiprecious gemstone has only one or two of these qualities. A **gem** is a gemstone that has been cut and polished.

Some minerals can be very beautiful, but they may be too soft and may scratch easily—such as fluorite. Most gemstones have a hardness on the Mohs' scale above 5 and a high index of refraction (the higher the index of refraction, the greater the sparkle). All natural gemstones,

Mohs' Scale

10	Diamond
9	Corundum (ruby, sapphire)
8	Topaz
7	Quartz
6.5	*Glass*
6	Potassium feldspar
5.5	*Pocketknife*
5	Apatite
4.5	*Teeth, bones*
4	Fluoride
3.5	*Penny*
3	Calcite
2.5	*Fingernail*
2	Gypsum
1	Talc

(Entries in italics are common items that are included for comparison to where the minerals fall in the hardness scale.)

however, have some characteristics falling short of perfection (only synthetic manmade gemstones are flawless).

Most gems are silicates, which can be very stable, hard minerals. A few gems are oxides, and only one gem—diamond—is composed of a single element (carbon). Diamond, corundum (ruby and sapphire), beryl (emerald and aquamarine), topaz, and opal are generally classed as precious stones. All other gemstones are usually classified as semiprecious.

Gemstones are not plentiful; they tend to be scattered sparsely throughout a large body of rock or to have crystallized as small veins.

Red Horn Coral

Red horn coral is a very rare, fossilized coral. It was created 65 to 85 million years ago (mya) and is found in the Uinta Mountains of Utah. During the Middle to Late Cretaceous period, 65 to 135 mya, the Earth's volcanic activity forced new ridge systems to rise high above the old ocean depths in the Pacific Ocean and lift neighboring ocean floors with them.

Not only was the ocean floor crust rising, but also massive amounts of carbon dioxide were released into the atmosphere because of all the volcanic activity, causing additional warming. The effect was dramatic; the icecaps melted, and the oceans were 656 feet (200 meters) higher than they are today.

The sea progressed inland up through the midwestern parts of the United States and almost into Canada, while much of Europe was underwater as well. The sea covered much of the Rocky Mountains, and because of the warming of the Earth's climate, it made an excellent habitat for the coral to live in.

The fossilized coral is a beautiful gemstone used in jewelry today. It ranges in color from pinks to deep reds and commonly has a starburst ray pattern running from the center to the edges. The coral gets its name from the horn-shaped formations it grew in.

The average grade of the richest diamond kimberlite pipes in Africa is about 1 part diamond in 40 million parts ore. Kimberlite, which is a plutonic **igneous rock**, ascends from a depth of at least 60 miles (100 kilometers) to form a diatreme (a narrow, cone-shaped rock body or "pipe"). Also, because most diamond is not of gem quality, the average stone in an engagement ring is the product of the removal and processing of 200 to 400 million times its volume of rock.

Gemstones occur in most major geologic environments. Each environment has specific gemstones suited to it, but some gems occur in more than one environment. Most gemstones are found in igneous rocks and alluvial gravels, but sedimentary and metamorphic rocks may also contain gem materials.

There are also organic gemstones, specifically four groups that are highly prized for their beauty and rarity: amber, coral, jet, and pearl. They are not, however, as durable as gemstones from minerals.

Since 1935, the mining of gemstones in the United States has been almost entirely a recreational activity of mineral collectors and hobbyists. Several kinds of natural gemstones have been found in every state of the United States, but much larger deposits of the most precious kinds are found outside the United States. States containing the most gemstones include Tennessee, California, Arizona, Arkansas, Montana, Nevada, and Maine. According to the Arkansas Department of Parks, an estimated 80,000 visitors found a total of 315 **carats** of diamonds in the Crater of Diamonds State Park in Arkansas. Abundant yields of freshwater pearls come from Tennessee; turquoise is found in Arizona and Nevada; tourmaline exists in Maine; and tourmaline, kunzite, and garnet occur in California.

The United States produces pearl, garnet, jade, jasper, mother-of-pearl, opal, peridot, quartz, sapphire, tourmaline, and turquoise. Except for the few gem diamonds that are found each year in Arkansas, U.S. diamond production is very low, but exploration efforts continue today in Alaska, Colorado, Michigan, Minnesota, Wisconsin, and Wyoming.

World diamond reserves are estimated to be about 300 million carats, including near-gem materials, but this does not include diamonds

Red horn coral is very rare, found in a remote site on a mountaintop in Utah, in the Uinta Mountains. This area was once in a tropical biome under an ocean, which allowed the coral to form. It is found in small formations that look like horns. Crusted on the outside with deposits from an ancient sea, it is polished to reveal the beautiful coral inside. Each piece of coral has a unique design within it ranging from starburst shapes to clusters of curious bubbles. This rare coral is popular in custom jewelry. This photo shows a polished piece of natural red horn coral in the center, surrounded by custom-made coral pendants crafted by Navajo silversmiths. Each piece has its own unique pattern, which is not visible until the jeweler polishes it. *(Courtesy of Nature's Images)*

of abrasive quality. Most of the reserves are in southern Africa, Siberia, and western Australia.

Precious Metals

Precious metals, like gemstones, are classified in part by their rarity, which can impart a high economic value. Durability and ductility are also important characteristics. Durability keeps metal from corroding or becoming brittle. Ductility ensures that the metal is malleable—it can be bent, hammered, and shaped.

Gold is the most malleable of metals—it can be hammered into incredibly thin foils or drawn into extremely fine wires. It does not corrode or dissolve, except under the most extreme conditions. In fact, it is so durable that nearly all the gold ever mined is still in circulation or storage today.

The best-known precious metals are gold and silver. Although both metals have industrial uses, they are better known for their uses in art, jewelry, and coinage. Other precious metals include the platinum group metals (ruthenium, rhodium, palladium, osmium, iridium, and platinum). Plutonium and uranium could also be considered precious metals.

The demand for precious metals is driven not only by their practical use, but also by their role as investments. For value comparisons, in May of 2006, palladium was $371 (U.S. dollars) per ounce; gold was $682 per ounce; platinum was $1,188 per ounce; and silver was $13.93 per ounce. Valuable precious metals can make good investments.

The Difference Between *Carat* and *Karat*

Although they are pronounced the same way, a *carat* and a *karat* are not the same thing. A carat is the standard unit of weight for gemstones. One carat equals 0.2 grams (0.007 oz.).

A karat is a measure of the purity of gold alloys. One karat equals 1/24 pure gold. Pure gold is 24 karat, often written 24k. Eighteen-karat gold, written 18k, contains 18 parts gold mixed with 6 parts of another metal. Likewise, 12k gold contains 12 parts gold and 12 parts of another metal. Metals are added to gold to make it more durable because gold is a relatively soft metal.

WHERE MINERALS ARE FOUND

Natural minerals are not evenly distributed in the Earth's crust. Concentrations of mineral resources that are profitable to extract are found only in specific areas; a special set of circumstances must have occurred in or on the Earth to create mineral deposits. Three things had to exist: there had to be a supply of certain elements available in the Earth, a process to concentrate them, and a host rock to trap the mineral or minerals. Many minerals commonly occur together, such as quartz and gold; molybdenum, tin, and tungsten; copper, lead, and zinc; and platinum and palladium.

The signs of a mineral deposit are often small and difficult to recognize. Sometimes geologists must search for years before finding an economically profitable mineral deposit. Deposit size, mineral content, extraction efficiency and costs all determine if a mineral resource can be profitably developed. If it is too expensive to retrieve and process, it will not make a profit.

Ores can be found in many different types of rock—igneous, metamorphic, and sedimentary—but the processes that form the deposits can vary from rock to rock. Some minerals form inside magma chambers, and others form near igneous activity.

Magma chambers are large bodies of molten rock that form within the Earth's crust. Some concentrations of metals occur inside the magma and are found within **granites**. When magma begins to cool, crystals begin forming. The initial crystals that form are **feldspars**. Pegmatites—rocks with large crystals—then form. These are an important source of many rare metals and some gemstones. Carbonates can form in rocks rich in calcium—they can also contain rare metals. Other magma deposits can contain concentrations of just one type of mineral. Vanadium—an element used as an additive in steel to produce specialty stainless steel surgical instruments and which is also used in jet engines—is often formed this way.

When hot liquids boil off from the magma, they seep into surrounding fractures in rock. The hot liquid is able to transport **native**

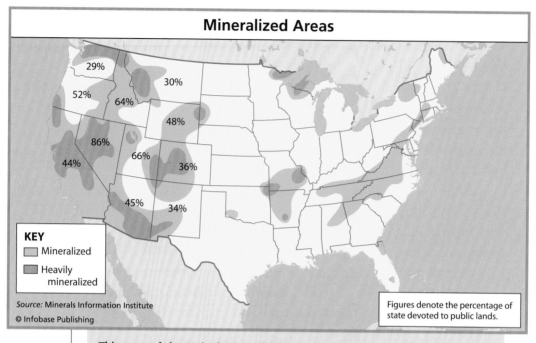

Mineralized Areas

29%
30%
52%
64%
48%
86%
44%
66%
36%
45%
34%

KEY
☐ Mineralized
☐ Heavily mineralized

Source: Minerals Information Institute
© Infobase Publishing

Figures denote the percentage of state devoted to public lands.

This map of the United States illustrates the locations of mineralized areas. Minerals are distributed unevenly across geographical locations.

metals (metals that occur uncombined with any other elements) and compounds into nearby fractures. These mineral-laden solutions are called hydrothermal fluids. These fluids usually exit via the surface of the ground, but sometimes they become trapped in the rocks and minerals begin to form. When this happens, the solutions both cool and solidify, or they react with minerals in the surrounding rocks.

Mineral deposits are also associated with volcanoes. If a volcano erupts underwater and it interacts with the seawater, a hydrothermal solution is produced and **sulfides** are created. This phenomenon can also be seen at hot springs on land (such as those at Yellowstone National Park).

A large deposit of a significant mineral is referred to as a lode. Many of the famous gold and silver rushes in the 1800s in California, Nevada, and Alaska were centered on famous lodes. Lodes can contain

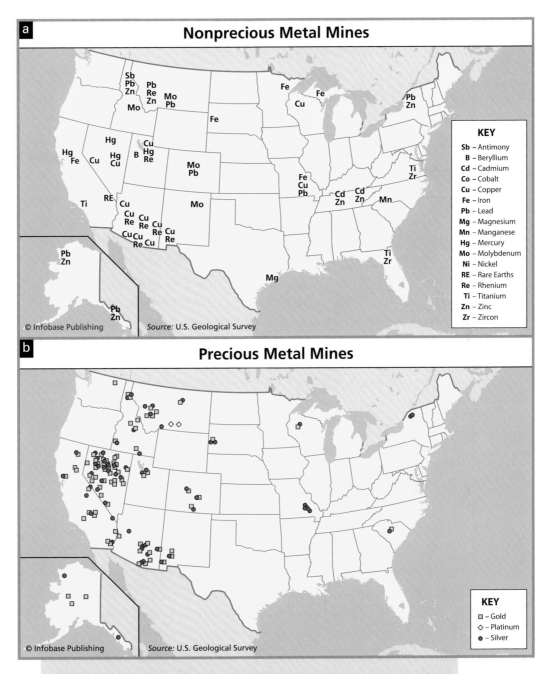

Different mineral commodities found within the United States: (a) nonprecious metals; (b) precious metals.

a variety of commodities, depending on their location, including gold, silver, copper, zinc, tin, lead, nickel, and uranium.

Minerals are also deposited when lakes or seas dry out. The dissolved minerals form layers on the dried-out bed, and their buildup year after year creates thick beds of salt, soda ash, borax, and other minerals. These are often called evaporite deposits. Lake Bonneville in Utah is one example of a famous ancient lake that evaporated and left abundant mineral deposits within extensive salt flats. The Great Salt Lake is the only remnant of the ancient lake, but evaporates and other minerals are substantial enough to support successful mining and extraction ventures.

Petroleum deposits are often found on seabed sediments, which is why major oil companies operate offshore drilling rigs. Petroleum exists in sedimentary rocks as either a liquid or a solid and develops from the decomposing bodies of microscopic sea life. Petroleum includes both oil and natural gas. Most petroleum deposits appear as a mixture of both liquids and gases. Petroleum is a useful product for much more than just a fuel; it is used extensively for manufacturing plastic, fibers, paints, and fertilizers.

Most petroleum reservoirs are located in pools called petroleum fields. They can range in size from very small up to tens of miles (km). They can also be hundreds of feet (m) deep. Petroleum geologists find petroleum deposits in **permeable rock** formations—rocks with enough open pore space to store the petroleum. These formations are often referred to as **reservoir rocks**. The best geologic structures for these are domes and tilted rocks that are closed by faults. Tilted rocks that have variable textures can serve as traps. Salt domes can also serve as traps.

If oil is stored in permeable rocks that have an outlet to the Earth's surface, light oil and natural gas will move upward and escape. The existence of active seeps like this tells geologists that more reserves may be located underground. Large areas of oil and natural gas occur in places where the rocks remain covered with an **impermeable** cap rock.

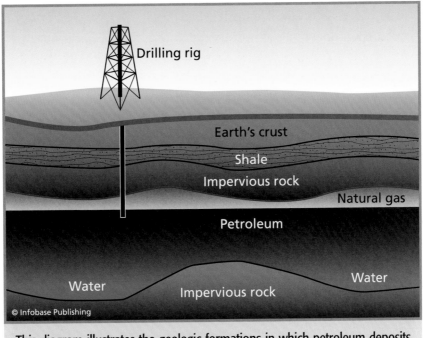

This diagram illustrates the geologic formations in which petroleum deposits are likely to occur. Natural gas forms on top of petroleum.

Minerals are also found in weathered soils in the tropics. In these areas, iron and aluminum oxides can be found. Soils that are mined for their aluminum content are called **bauxite**—the source of nearly all the Earth's aluminum.

Minerals can also be deposited by rivers and along coastal margins. These minerals are not concentrated where they formed. Instead, they are weathered from existing formations and then carried by water (rivers, waves, or currents) to other areas to be deposited. These types of deposits are called **placer deposits**. If the mineral reacts with the water, then it can be lost in solution; but if the mineral (such as gold, tin, magnetite iron, and diamonds) does not react, it will settle out of the water, be deposited, and become concentrated. Placer deposits have played a huge role in mineral development. In

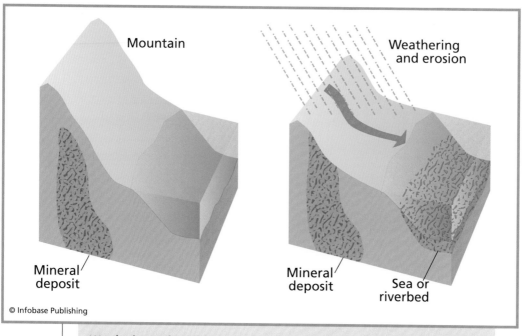

Mountain

Weathering and erosion

Mineral deposit

Mineral deposit

Sea or riverbed

© Infobase Publishing

Weathering and erosion can wash minerals down a slope and deposit them in a sea or riverbed.

fact, the majority of all the gold mined in the world has come from placer deposits.

MINERALS AND MATERIALS IN THE TWENTY-FIRST CENTURY

Metal ores can be found near igneous rocks in the cores of mountains or in some basins. The pattern of volcanic activity and mountain building influences the world distribution of minerals. Deposits are also concentrated into specific geologic time periods when the physical conditions needed to produce the mineral were met. For example, in addition to the Carboniferous period for coal formation, huge amounts of iron were deposited 2.5 to 1.8 billion years ago. Geologists try to find possible prospective coal and iron formations deposited during these identified time periods.

According to the U.S. Geological Survey (USGS), in the United States there are 1,879 coal mines and facilities, 8 uranium mines, and 1,965 mines and processing plants for 74 types of nonfuel minerals and materials. In spite of its size and mineral wealth, however, the United States is not able to produce all the minerals it needs to be self-sufficient. In order to maintain our lifestyle and provide all the present consumer products and facilities we use every day, various amounts of minerals must be imported from foreign countries.

THE HISTORY OF MINERALS AND THEIR IMPACT ON CIVILIZATION

Archaeological evidence indicates that, from their earliest steps toward advanced civilization, humans have used naturally occurring mineral materials to protect and improve their lives; and, throughout time, people have come to rely more and more on minerals. The standard of living we have today would not be possible without mining. Over the centuries, mining and minerals have contributed to the social, cultural, and economic advancement of human civilization and lifestyles.

Ancient people used many minerals from the Earth. For example, they used chert, flint, jasper, obsidian, and quartzite to make tools and weapons. They used clay to make pots for cooking and jars to hold water or food. Other minerals were used to obtain the coloring for the clay, which turned many pots into valuable pieces of artwork. The Anasazi tribe of the Southwest, which reached its peak of development in about A.D. 1000, is well known for its intricately painted clay pots.

Past civilizations also used various minerals, such as jade and turquoise, for trading, or bartering. Possession of gems was also an indicator of wealth. Building materials from minerals, such as soil, clay, and other materials to make adobe, were also used by past civilizations.

Historians have divided human history into several periods based on which metals were used during each period, such as the Stone Age (premetallic), which was followed by the Bronze Age in about 3000 B.C., during which people learned to make tools out of bronze. During the Iron Age—from 1500 to 1000 B.C.—people began to use iron to make stronger tools.

Many minerals have directly affected human lives. One example is salt. Salt has been prized for thousands of years. Not only does salt add flavor to food, it has also been used for centuries to prevent spoiling. Salt used to be so valuable that it was actually used as money in some countries. Roman soldiers were paid with salt. In fact, the word *salary* came from the Latin word *salarium*, which means "salt money." Salt is inexpensive now, but in ancient times it was just as valuable as gold.

This chapter discusses the various major developments in civilization and their connection to minerals. It also examines the world's most famous gold rushes; historical mining in the United States; prospecting today; and the uses of minerals, elements, and materials in the twentieth century.

THE STONE AGE

The Stone Age—also called the Paleolithic era—refers to a prehistoric time period during which humans widely used stone for tool making between 1.5 million and 20,000 years ago. It began with the creation of crude stone tools. This was the earliest age in which humans began to build a working knowledge of weapons and utensils carved from stone. It designates a premetallurgic period whose stone tools proved more durable than those made previously from softer materials.

Tools were made from several different types of stone. For example, chert and flint were chipped (shaped) for use as cutting tools and

During the Stone Age, tools and weapons (such as arrowheads) were made of stones such as obsidian. Pottery was crafted from clay and often painted in beautiful, intricate designs. Colors for the pottery were derived from minerals and organic materials. *(Courtesy of Nature's Images)*

weapons, while **basalt** and **sandstone** were used for ground stone tools, such as quern-stones used for grinding grain. Wood, bone, antler, and shell were also used to make tools and weapons. During the later parts of this age, humans learned how to use natural sediments such as clay to make crude pottery.

The Stone Age is significant because it represents the first known widespread use of technology in human history and the consequent spread of civilization from East Africa to the rest of the world. The Stone Age ended when humans began to learn how to smelt copper ore to produce metal.

THE COPPER AGE

The Copper Age is the time period in which humans learned to create crude metallic tools. The Copper Age marks a significant transitional step in the progress of civilization and technology. The most notable locations of copper activity occurred in southeast Europe and western and central Asia in about 4000 B.C. Discoveries have shown that raw copper was being made into tools and ornaments as early as 10,000 B.C. in Yugoslavia. The Copper Age also affected American civilizations to a lesser degree. The Copper Age quickly made way for the Bronze Age once the process of alloying (combining metals) was utilized.

THE BRONZE AGE

The Bronze Age was the time in the development of human culture before the introduction of iron. Most tools and weapons during this age were made of bronze, which came into use at different times in different parts of the world. Its transition to, and replacement by, iron also occurred at different times in history in different geographical regions.

Archaeological discoveries since 1960 have changed many previous theories concerning the origins of copper and bronze technologies. Originally, historians thought that the use of bronze had originated in the Middle East; but discoveries near Ban Chiang, Thailand, indicate that bronze technology was in use there as early as 4500 B.C. Bronze objects have been found in Asia Minor that date from before 3000 B.C. Initially, this alloy was used sparingly—mostly for decorative purposes, because the tin needed to make it was not easy to obtain.

The first objects produced by ancient cultures included axes, knives, and agricultural tools. As artisans gained experience in bronze-working technology, they produced many ornate and highly decorative objects for administrative, religious, and other ceremonial purposes. The Bronze Age ended when iron technology was developed.

THE IRON AGE

The Iron Age was the stage of development in civilization in which humans began to use iron implements as tools and weapons. Just as in the previous ages, its dates of development vary by geographical location. For example, it began in the twelfth century B.C. in Greece, in the eleventh century B.C. in India, in the eighth century B.C. in central Europe, and the sixth century B.C. in northern Europe.

Iron's hardness and high melting point, as well as the abundance of iron ore sources, made iron more desirable and less expensive than bronze. The first uses of iron in Egypt were for the tips of spears and for decorative use. At that time, iron was an expensive metal, even more expensive than gold. Some experts believe that iron's discovery may have been because it was a by-product of copper refining. The earliest systematic production and use of iron implements appeared in India and then later became more common in other areas. By A.D. 200, high-quality steel was being produced in southern India by what Europeans would later name the "crucible" technique. A crucible is a container of metal used to heat substances to high temperatures. In this system, high-purity wrought iron, charcoal, and glass were mixed in crucibles and heated until the iron melted and absorbed the carbon. The resulting high-carbon steel was exported throughout much of Asia and Europe. Throughout history at that time, the use of iron weapons became extremely important. Iron was also crucial in tools and equipment used in early farming practices.

THE INDUSTRIAL REVOLUTION

The Industrial Revolution was the major technological, socioeconomic, and cultural change in the late eighteenth and early nineteenth centuries that began in Britain and spread to Western Europe, North America, and then throughout the world. This marks the time in history when an economy based on manual labor was replaced by one dominated by industry and the manufacture of machinery. This revolution began with the mechanization of the textile industries and the development of iron-making techniques. Trade expansion was made possible by the introduction of canals, improved roads, and railways, which were necessary to transport products to markets. The introduction of steam power (which was fueled by coal) and powered machinery was responsible for the rapid mechanization and development of society. The use of minerals was critical in allowing the rapid developments that occurred, which led to the lifestyle that developed countries enjoy today.

During the Industrial Revolution, steam-powered ships and railways were developed followed by the internal combustion engine and electrical power generation. The invention of the steam engine is considered one of the most important innovations of the Industrial Revolution. This was made possible by earlier improvements in iron **smelting** and metalworking, based on the use of coke (a product from coal) rather than charcoal. Several industries made advancements during this time period—mining, metallurgy, steam power, factories, machine tools, and transportation, to name a few.

In mining, the introduction of the steam engine greatly facilitated the removal of water and enabled **shafts** to be dug deeper, enabling more minerals to be extracted. Improvements in machine tools increased productivity, and iron became a major construction material used in the building of large structures, such as bridges.

In 1769, James Watt created the Watt steam engine. His invention improved engine efficiency, which saved 75% on coal costs. The Watt steam engine's ability to drive rotary machinery enabled it to be used to drive a factory or mill directly. Also, the development of planing and shaping machines powered by these engines enabled all the metal parts of the engines to be consistently and accurately cut, which made it possible to build larger and more powerful engines.

Industrialization led to the creation of the factory, where raw materials went in at one end, were smelted, and were turned into pots, tools, wire, and other useful goods. The factory system was largely responsible for the rise of the modern city, because workers quickly moved into cities in order to be close to the factories where they worked.

GOLD RUSHES

A gold rush is a period of rapid migration of miners into an area where commercial quantities of gold have been discovered. During the 1800s, many gold rushes took place in the United States, Canada, Australia, New Zealand, and Africa. These became some of the most famous gold rushes in history. In North America, gold rushes attracted a huge number of settlers who then ended up contributing to the culture of the locations in which they lived. During this time period, money was based on gold, so there was also a significant economic incentive to locate newly mined gold.

The first real gold rush in the United States occurred in the Appalachian Mountains during the 1830s. The California gold rush of 1848–1849 in the Sierra Nevada then followed, with multitudes of settlers rushing to the American West. The California gold rush spurred the rapid settlement of California by Americans, which resulted in the area becoming an official state in 1850, when it was admitted into the Union.

Several gold rushes occurred in North America, particularly in the American West; they then moved northward through the Rocky Mountain area and into British Columbia, Canada. A gold rush typically began with the discovery of "free gold" by a single individual. These types of finds were generally placer gold in the beds of streams that descend from a nearby mountain range. The word quickly got out and spread.

The result was always the same—the discovery spurred the immediate influx of other prospectors who rushed to the area to either join existing prospecting groups or to form new ones. The reality was that the so-called free gold supply in these placer claims would soon become depleted, and the initial frenzied phase would be replaced by a longer period of prospecting in the upper canyon walls for the lode gold (the main body of the gold deposit).

A gold rush usually lasted only a few years. Sometimes in these mining communities, if the geologic conditions were right, the mining area would transition to further calculated prospecting and mining for silver. The California gold rush spanned a period of time from 1848 to 1858. It started at Sutter's Mill near Coloma, California, on January 24, 1848, when James W. Marshall (an employee of Sacramento agriculturist John Sutter) found a gold nugget. Prospecting quickly expanded northward where gold nuggets were also discovered in Yreka, California.

Perhaps the biggest highlight of the gold rush era was the Klondike (it is often referred to as "the last grand adventure" by the National Park Service). Much of this era is brought to life in Jack London's famous novels, *Call of the Wild* and *White Fang*. The Klondike began in 1896, when three men—Skookum Jim Mason, Dawson Charlie, and George Washington Carmack—found gold in a tributary of the Klondike River in Canada's Yukon Territory. Their discovery set off the greatest gold rush in history.

Beginning in 1897, a hoard of hopeful gold seekers—unaware that most of the good Klondike claims were already staked—boarded ships at Seattle and other Pacific port cities and headed north in search of riches that were said to be had for the taking. All through the summer and into the winter of 1897–1898, stampeders poured into the newly created Alaskan tent and shack towns of Skagway and Dyea. These ports were the beginning points for the 600-mile (966 km) trek to the fabled goldfields.

A former steamboat captain named William Moore founded Skagway, which is located at the head of the White Pass Trail. His small homestead was inundated with about 10,000 transient residents struggling to get their required year's worth of gear and supplies over the Coast Range and down the Yukon River headwaters at lakes Lindeman and Bennett. Dyea, at the head of Taiya Inlet, experienced the same boomtown commotion as gold seekers poured in and picked their way up the Chilkoot Trail into Canada.

During this famous and historic trek, the gold stampeders faced their greatest hardships on the Chilkoot Trail and the White Pass Trail.

Elusive Gold and Myths

Many myths and ancient beliefs originated from different minerals, crystals, and gemstones. Throughout history, people have been fascinated by gold. Dreams of gaining immense wealth and uncovering enormous lost treasures have captured the attention of many. In fact nearly every culture has its own myths associated with gold. For example, consider these:

- *Blackbeard's Gold:* Blackbeard was a famous pirate in the early 1700s who sailed the waters near Virginia, North Carolina and South Carolina. Many people claim he buried a large treasure chest of gold somewhere nearby. To this day, it has never been discovered.
- *El Dorado:* El Dorado is the fabled "Lost City of Gold." The Spanish Conquistadors set out to find it in the 1500s. Their leaders kept pushing them north, all the way to what is presently the state of New Mexico, in their futile search for this legendary city.
- *The Golden Chariot:* Gold is an obsession in ancient Greek myths, as well. According to legend, a young man named Phaethon was flying his father's golden chariot and lost control. The impact on the earth from the crashed chariot is what created the present Libyan Desert.
- *King Midas and the Golden Touch:* The Greco-Roman myth of Midas is about a king who wished that everything he

There were murders, suicides, disease, malnutrition, and death from hypothermia and avalanches. The Chilkoot Trail was the toughest because it was too difficult for pack animals to carry supplies on the steep slopes leading to the pass. Until tramways were built late in 1897 and early 1898, the stampeders had to carry everything on their own backs. The White Pass Trail was known as the animal killer, because anxious prospectors overloaded and beat their pack animals and forced

touched would turn to gold. Unfortunately for King Midas, the god Dionysus made the king's wish come true. Midas soon regretted his foolish wish and begged Dionysus to take the spell off.

- *The Wind River Gold:* This legend takes place in the American West. One day, three prospectors in the Wind River Mountains found some large nuggets of gold in the streams they were working. Local Indians attacked and killed two of the men, but the third one escaped. Later, when he went back to retrieve the gold from a cabin in which the gold had been hidden, the cabin had mysteriously disappeared. According to the legend, the gold is still out in the wilderness somewhere.

- *Lost Gold of the Uintas:* Legend has it that, in the rugged Uinta Mountains of northern Utah, Spanish explorers brought great quantities of stolen Aztec gold and hid it in secret caves. Trees in the area have secret symbols carved on them, leading the way to the hiding places. Scores of treasure hunters look for the lost gold each spring, summer, and fall before the harsh winter settles in. The lost gold has never been found.

VIEW SHOWING THE MODE OF TRAVEL ON THE CHILKOOT.

Klondikers at "the Scales," ascending the Chilkoot Pass, Alaska, in 1898, during the Klondike gold rush. This viewpoint is about halfway up the pass looking down on the Scales. *(Photo by Eric A. Hegg, University of Washington Libraries, Special Collections Division)*

them over the rocky terrain until they dropped. More than 3,000 animals died on this trail; many of their bones still lie at the bottom of Dead Horse Gulch.

During the first year of the rush, an estimated 20,000 to 30,000 gold seekers spent an average of three months packing their supplies up the trails and over the passes to the lakes in extremely difficult conditions. The distance from tidewater to the lake was only about 35 miles (56 km), but each individual trudged hundreds of miles back and forth along the trails, moving his gear from cache to cache. Once the prospectors had hauled all their gear to the lakes, they built, or bought, boats to float the remaining 560 miles (901 km) downriver to Dawson

City and the Klondike mining district where an almost limitless supply of gold nuggets was said to lie.

By midsummer of 1898, there were 18,000 people at Dawson, with more than 5,000 working the diggings. By August, many of the

Placers

A placer is a surface mineral deposit formed by the mechanical concentration of heavy minerals eroded from weathered rock masses by currents in streams, along beaches, or by wind. Many types of valuable minerals, including gold, platinum, cassiterite, ilmenite, zircon, rutile, sapphire, ruby, and diamond, are much denser than the average sand or sediment in an area. When air or water currents move these sediments, the heavy minerals tend to be concentrated by several processes. Denser grains become trapped in riffles, cracks, and in areas of low-flow velocity where they can settle out. For the placer minerals to be concentrated, they must also be resistant to chemical weathering, mechanical abrasion, and fragmentation during transport to keep from being destroyed. Famous alluvial placer deposits include the California and Klondike alluvial gold deposits, the sites of the famous gold rushes of the later half of the 1800s.

The largest gold placer deposit in the world is an ancient, 2.6- to 2.7-billion-year-old paleoplacer system found in the Witwatersrand basin of South Africa. It has accounted for nearly half of the world's production of gold. Beach placers include the diamonds found in ancient offshore beach deposits off southwest Africa; gold in beach ridges near Nome, Alaska; and placers along the southeast shores of Madagascar. An additional class of placers includes colluvial deposits, in which weathered material accumulates on a slope.

Placer mining is one of the oldest forms of mining. Running water is used to wash away the less-dense material, leaving the gold behind. Placer mining has been responsible for the production of much of the world's gold, tin, titanium, platinum, diamonds, rubies, emeralds, and sapphires.

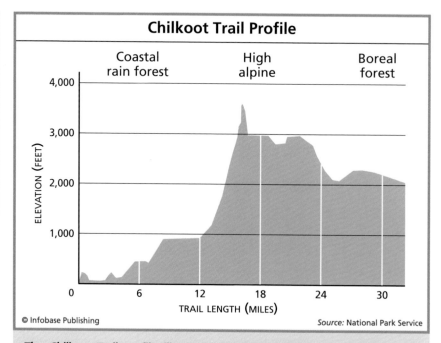

Chilkoot Trail Profile

The Chilkoot Trail profile illustrates the drastic changes in elevations the prospectors had to negotiate—much of it done in severe winterlike conditions. Each gold seeker was required to have a year's worth of supplies before being allowed to proceed to the Klondike from coastal ports in Alaska, such as Skagway.

stampeders had started for home, most of them broke. The next year saw a still larger exodus of miners leaving the area. The great Klondike gold rush ended as suddenly as it had begun.

THE USES OF ELEMENTS IN MODERN SOCIETY

Maintaining our standard of living requires the continual production of raw materials. Those materials provide people with food, homes, transportation, schools, hospitals, factories, and the equipment and energy necessary to make them operate.

In 1776, when the United States became an independent nation, people's needs were much more simple, requiring fewer natural resources. Most people never traveled more than 20 miles (32 km) from where they were born. Today, more than 200 years later, times have greatly changed. In order to maintain our current standard of living, raw materials must be found, mined, and processed each day in much greater amounts than ever before and the need continues to rise. For example, the table below compares the average amounts of materials used in 1776 per person in the United States versus the amounts used today.

Historical and Modern Usage of Minerals

Commodity used	Annual pounds/(kilograms) in 1776 by the average American	Annual pounds/(kilograms) used today by each American
Aluminum (bauxite)	0 pounds (0 kilograms)	80 pounds (36 kg)
Cement	12 pounds (5 kg)	904 pounds (410 kg)
Clay	100 pounds (45 kg)	290 pounds (132 kg)
Coal	40 pounds (18 kg)	7,410 pounds (3,361 kg)
Copper	1 pound (0.5 kg)	20 pounds (9 kg)
Iron ore	20 pounds (9 kg)	441 pounds (200 kg)
Lead	2 pounds (0.9 kg)	11 pounds (5 kg)
Phosphate	0 pounds (0 kg)	327 pounds (148 kg)
Potash	1 pound (0.5 kg)	43 pounds (20 kg)
Salt	4 pounds (2 kg)	405 pounds (184 kg)
Sand, gravel, stone	1,000 pounds (454 kg)	21,640 pounds (9,816 kg)
Sulfur	1 pound (0.5 kg)	93 pounds (42 kg)
Zinc	0.5 pounds (0.2 kg)	11 pounds (5 kg)

Source: Mineral Information Institute

According to the Mineral Information Institute, many things have changed in the nonfuel minerals industry over the past 100 years alone. At the beginning of the 1900s, some minerals and metals industries were well established, such as those for copper, gold, lead, lime, and salt; some industries were just beginning, such those for aluminum and lithium; and some materials, such as germanium, magnesium, and titanium, had not yet been commercially produced. Mining was labor intensive and could be dangerous. In 1900, U.S. mineral consumption was less than 110 million tons (100 million metric tons). By 2000, U.S. mineral consumption had increased to more than 3.6 billion tons (3.3 billion metric tons) and included not only the materials that constitute the bulk of the consumption—crushed stone and steel—but also some of the materials for which there were no uses in 1900.

CLASSES OF MINERALS

There are two general classes of resources: renewable and non-renewable. A renewable resource is a resource that can be replenished. It is a resource that can be replaced by natural ecological cycles, Earth system cycles, and good management practices. The opposite of this is a nonrenewable resource—a resource that cannot be replenished (once it is gone, it is gone for good). For practical applications, scientists consider a renewable resource as one that can be replenished within one generation (about 20–30 years). Although the same geologic processes that formed nonrenewable resources such as fossil fuels and nuclear energy are still working on Earth today, they take millions of years to form, so they are not considered renewable resources for the present life on Earth.

MINERALS ARE NONRENEWABLE

Mineral resources make modern life possible. Minerals are nonrenewable, however. Although the processes that created minerals are still actively occurring today, it takes hundreds, thousands, even millions of years in some cases for them to form. For some minerals, it took special geologic conditions in order for their formation to occur, and they may not be actively forming today because those conditions are not being met. The

Common Types of Habit, Luster, and Fracture

Note: A complete listing of mineral habits, fractures, and luster is listed in the Appendix.

Types of habit (The characteristic crystal form or combination of forms of a mineral)
- Acicular–occurs as needlelike crystals
- Bladed–aggregates of thin lathlike crystals
- Botryoidal–grapelike rounded forms
- Columnar–forms columns
- Encrustations–forms crustlike aggregates on matrix
- Dendritic–branching treelike growths of great complexity
- Foliated–two-dimensional platy forms
- Lamellar–thin laminae producing a lamellar structure
- Massive–fibrous–distinctly fibrous fine-grained forms
- Massive–granular–common texture observed in granite and other igneous rock
- Nodular–tuberose forms having irregular protuberances over the surface
- Prismatic–crystals shaped like slender prisms
- Reniform–kidneylike in shape
- Scale–thin fragments
- Stalactitic–shaped like pendant columns as stalactites or stalagmites

Types of luster (The reflection of light from the surface of a mineral)
- Adamantine–high index of refraction
- Adamantine–greasy–between adamantine and greasy

mineral resources we use today were created long ago, and once we have used them all, there will not be anymore within the near future.

The minerals we depend on are not renewable, so it is important that our use of them be responsible and sustainable. Besides benefiting

- Adamantine–metallic–between adamantine and metallic
- Adamantine–pearly–between pearly and adamantine
- Adamantine–resinous–between resinous and adamantine
- Adamantine–silky–between silky and adamantine
- Earthy (dull)–complete dull
- Greasy (oily)–surface alteration
- Metallic–specular reflection
- Pearly–formed by numerous partly developed cleavages
- Silky–noticeable shiny direction
- Translucent–allows light to pass through
- Transparent–can clearly be seen through
- Vitreous–luster of broken glass

Types of fracture (The way in which a mineral breaks)
- Conchoidal–fractures developed in brittle materials characterized by smoothly curving surfaces
- Hackly–shows jagged points in fracture
- Regular–flat surfaces (not cleavage) fractured in a regular pattern
- Subconchoidal–fractures developed in brittle materials characterized by semicurving surfaces
- Uneven–flat surfaces (not cleavage) fractured in an uneven pattern

(Source: U.S. Geological Survey)

from the use of these natural resources, we also have an obligation to manage and plan for the environmental and social impacts associated with mining and processing. It is important to use these nonrenewable resources in a sustainable way to ensure that the benefit of using those resources now is balanced with the importance of saving those resources for future generations.

The way we use, supply, and manage these nonrenewable resources is critical and plays an important role in every person's life. It has been estimated by experts that in an average human lifetime, the average American will use the following mineral resources:

- 32,061 pounds (14,543 kg) of salt
- 1.64 million pounds (743,891 kg) of stone, sand, and gravel
- 81,585 gallons (308,832 liters) of petroleum
- 68,110 pounds (30,894 kg) of cement
- 57,448 pounds (26,058 kg) of other minerals and metals
- 5.9 million cubic feet (167 cubic decameter) of natural gas
- 45,176 pounds (20,491 kg) of iron ore
- 1,074 pounds (487 kg) of lead
- 5,599 pounds (10,750 kg) of aluminum
- 23,700 pounds (10,740 kg) of phosphates
- 586,218 pounds (265,904 kg) of coal
- 2.196 troy ounces (62256 milligrams) of gold
- 1,841 pounds (835 kg) of copper
- 21,476 pounds (9,741 kg) of clay
- 997 pounds (452 kg) of zinc

Source: Mineral Information Institute

Minerals can be classified according to their chemical composition and crystal structure and can be subdivided into 10 types of classes: (1) elements, (2) sulfides, (3) halides, (4) oxides, (5) carbonates, (6) sulfates, (7) phosphates, (8) silicates, (9) organics, and (10) **mineraloids**.

THE ELEMENTS CLASS

Some elements can be found on their own and uncombined with other elements because they are not very reactive. They are known as native metals and include gold, silver, platinum, and copper. They can be found as veins—narrow cracks filled with minerals—that cut through other rocks. Because they do not require any processing to separate them from other elements, native metals are easy to use.

Ancient civilizations used native metals extensively because the processes used to separate the metals from ores did not exist at that time.

The Value of Aluminum and Gold

Aluminum
Abundant and versatile, aluminum is now cheap and widely available, but that has not always been the case. Early in the nineteenth century, the French emperor Napoleon III served food to his royal guests on aluminum plates. Aluminum—the most abundant metal in the Earth's crust—was once very precious because, in the early 1800s, aluminum was extremely difficult to remove from rocks and, therefore, was considered very valuable. In 1886, when an inexpensive method of extraction was developed, aluminum suddenly became cheap and widely available.

Gold
Glittering and durable, gold has historically been a symbol of wealth and power. Yet today, gold is a workhorse metal for high technology. Why is gold so valuable? Gold is scarce. Throughout history, only about 128,000 tons (116,000 metric tons) have been found—enough to make a cube about 59 feet (18 m) on a side. Gold is beautiful. Ancient cultures equated its brilliance with the sun, and today it is still prized for its glow in jewelry and ornaments. Gold has properties valuable to industry, such as excellent electrical conductivity and corrosion resistance.

(Source: National Museum of Natural History)

Today, that is not a problem because techniques to do this have been perfected over the years. To be useful, native metals need to occur in large pieces, which is rare. When they do occur in large pieces, they can lead the discoverer to great wealth (such as a large body of gold). Native elements are free, uncombined elements which are classified in three groups: (1) metals, such as gold, silver, and copper; (2) semimetals, including arsenic and antimony; and (3) nonmetals, such as carbon and sulfur.

Metallic elements are very dense, soft, malleable (can be shaped), ductile, and opaque. It is common for them to have branchlike habits (characteristic appearance). Distinct crystals are rare.

Unlike metals, semimetals are poor conductors of electricity, and they usually occur in nodular (clumped) masses. Nonmetallic elements are transparent to translucent, do not conduct electricity, and tend to form distinct crystals.

Native elements represent a fairly small group—there are only about 50 members. Some—such as gold and silver—are rare and commercially valuable. Other native elements include platinum, bismuth, arsenic, copper, sulfur, silicon, mercury, and antimony.

THE SULFIDES CLASS

Sulfides are chemical compounds in which sulfur has combined with metallic and semimetallic elements. These are some of the most important compounds that produce useful ores. The compound is called a sulfide. Common sulfides include pyrite (iron sulfide—commonly known as fool's gold), chalcopyrite (copper iron sulfide), pentlandite (nickel iron sulfide), and galena (lead sulfide).

Oftentimes these metals occur together so that the mining of one or more makes it easy to obtain the others. For instance, indium and cadmium are produced almost entirely as by-products of zinc sulfide smelting. Many sulfides have metallic lusters and are soft and dense— such as galena and molybdenite. Some are nonmetallic or relatively hard. Sulfides usually have well-formed, highly symmetrical crystals.

Native elements, such as gold, silver, platinum, and copper, as well as lead, zinc, nickel, molybdenum, arsenic, antimony, bismuth, cobalt,

Chalcopyrite is a copper iron sulfide mineral that crystallizes in the tetragonal system. Chalcopyrite is one of the most important copper ores. *(Photo courtesy of Nature's Images)*

and mercury, can all form sulfide ores. They form in hydrothermal veins below the water table where they are easily oxidized to sulfates. Sulfosalts are compounds in which metallic elements combine with sulfur plus a semimetallic element (such as antimony and arsenic). Their properties are similar to those of sulfides.

There are many uses for sulfides. For example, cadmium sulfide is used in photocells, and calcium polysulfide ("lime sulfur") is used in gardening. Carbon disulfide is used as a solvent; lead sulfide is used in infrared sensors; sodium sulfide is used as an industrial chemical to make dyes, in crude petroleum processing, and in leather tanning; and zinc sulfide is used for photo luminescent strips for emergency lighting and luminous watch dials.

Calcite on fluorite (carbonate/halide). Fluorite is a halide and is used in making opalescent glass, enamels for cooking utensils, and as a flux in the manufacture of steel. *(Photo courtesy of Nature's Images)*

THE HALIDES CLASS

Halides are compounds in which metallic elements combine with halogens. The halide class includes the fluoride, chloride, bromine, and iodide minerals. The most familiar halide mineral is **halite** (NaCl) or rock salt. One of the most colorful minerals is fluorite. It is prized for its glassy luster and rich variety of colors. The range of common colors for fluorite include purple, blue, green, yellow, brown, pink, black, reddish orange, and colorless.

Halides are common in many geologic environments. They are the group of minerals forming the natural salts. Some, such as halite, are found as evaporite deposits in areas like playa lake beds and landlocked seas such as the Dead Sea in the Middle East and the Great Salt Lake in

Utah. Some halides are found in alternating layers of sedimentary rock, which contain evaporites, such as **gypsum**, halite, and potash rock, interbedded with rocks such as marl and limestone.

Other halides—like fluorite—occur in hydrothermal veins. Halides are usually very soft minerals, and many have cubic crystal symmetry. Their specific gravity tends to be low.

THE OXIDES CLASS

Another group of common compounds that produce useful ores is the oxides. An oxide is a metal that exists in combination with oxygen. In fact, aluminum, chromium, iron, manganese, tin, titanium, and uranium are mainly found in the form of oxides. Oxides are extremely important in mining because they form many of the ores from which valuable metals can be extracted. Oxides form a diverse group, occurring in many geologic environments and in most rock types. They commonly occur in three ways: (1) as precipitates close to the Earth's surface, (2) oxidation products of other minerals in the near-surface-weathering zone, and (3) as accessory minerals in igneous rocks of the crust and mantle. Common oxides include hematite (iron oxide), magnetite (iron oxide), chromite (chromium oxide), spinel (magnesium aluminum oxide, a component of the Earth's mantle), rutile (titanium dioxide), and ice (hydrogen oxide).

Some oxides, such as hematite, magnetite, cassiterite, and chromite are important ores of metals. Others, like corundum, have gemstone varieties such as ruby and sapphire. The properties of the oxides are varied. The gem varieties and metallic ores are very hard and have a high specific gravity. They also vary considerably in color, from the rich red of ruby to the blue of sapphire and from the red, green, and blue of spinel to the black of magnetite.

THE CARBONATES CLASS

Carbonates are compounds in which one or more metallic or semi-metallic elements combine with the CO_3^{2-} carbonate radical. It is a combination of metal with carbon and oxygen. Although **carbonate**

Agate (oxide) is a term applied to an aggregate of various forms of silica. Some cultures have certain beliefs about agates. In Islam, agates are deemed to be very precious stones. According to tradition, the wearer of an agate ring is believed to be protected from various mishaps and will enjoy longevity, among other benefits. In other traditions, agate is believed to cure the stings of scorpions and the bites of snakes, soothe the mind, prevent disease, still thunder and lightning, promote eloquence, secure the favor of the powerful, and bring victory over enemies. Persian magi are also known to have prized agate rings in their work and beliefs. *(Photo courtesy of Nature's Images)*

minerals—like manganese, iron, and magnesium—are common, they are more expensive to extract (compared to sulfides and oxides). This makes them a less desirable source of metal. Carbonates are usually deposited in marine settings when the shells of dead plankton settle and accumulate on the seafloor. Carbonates are also found in evaporitic settings (such as the Great Salt Lake in Utah) as well as karst regions, where the dissolution and reprecipitation of carbonates leads to the formation of caves, stalactites, and stalagmites. (Florida is known

Dog-tooth calcite (carbonate). Calcite is a common constituent of sedimentary rocks. It also occurs as a vein mineral in deposits from hot springs. *(Photo courtesy of Nature's Images)*

Malachite (carbonate) is a minor ore of copper and a common secondary mineral that is found in the oxidized zone of copper-sulfide deposits. It is used to make ornamental objects. *(Photo courtesy of Nature's Images)*

Selenite rose (sulfate). Selenite is soft and can easily be scratched with a fingernail. The thin crystals can be slightly flexible but will snap if bent too far. Some crystals grow in curved patterns and flowerlike petals. In dry desert conditions, sand may become trapped inside the crystals as they form. Sandy selenite formations can take on the shape of an hourglass or the more familiar "desert rose" shape. *(Photo courtesy of Nature's Images)*

for its diversity of karst landscapes.) The carbonate class also includes the nitrate and borate minerals.

THE SULFATES CLASS

Sulfates are compounds in which one or more metallic elements combine with the sulfate (SO_4^{2-}) radical. Gypsum, the most abundant sulfate, occurs in evaporite deposits. Barite usually occurs in hydrothermal veins. Most sulfates are soft, light in color, and not very dense. Chromates are compounds where metallic elements combine with the chromate (CrO_4^{2-}) radical. Chromates are rare and brightly colored. Molybdates and tungstates form when metallic elements combine with

Variscite (phosphate). A hydrated aluminum phosphate, it is a relatively rare phosphate mineral. Variscite is formed by direct deposition from phosphate-bearing water that has reacted with aluminum-rich rocks in a near-surface environment. Variscite is sometimes used as a semiprecious stone and is popular for carvings and ornamental use. *(Photo courtesy of Nature's Images)*

molybdate (MoO_4^{2-}) and tungstate (WO_4^{2-}) radicals. These are usually dense, brittle, and vividly colored minerals.

Sulfates form in evaporitic settings where extremely saline (salty) waters slowly evaporate, which allows the formation of both sulfates and halides where the sediments and water interact. They also occur in hydrothermal vein systems as **gangue** minerals along with sulfide ore minerals. Gangue is the unwanted rock that must be dug up in order to get to the commodity being mined.

Sulfates, also known as sulfur oxides, are important in both the chemical industry and biological systems. For example, they are used in lead-acid batteries, support deep-sea anaerobic microorganisms, are used as an agent to kill algae, and are used in therapeutic baths (these are called Epsom salts).

THE PHOSPHATES CLASS

Phosphates are compounds in which metallic elements combine with phosphate (PO_4^{3-}). Phosphates are not abundant. They are also soft, brittle, very colorful, and well crystallized. Phosphates include the radioactive minerals torbernite and autunite, lead-rich pyromorphite, bright blue lazulite, and turquoise. The most common phosphate is apatite, which is an important biological mineral found in the teeth and bones of many animals. Phosphates vary in hardness from 1.5 to 6.0 on Mohs' scale.

THE SILICATES CLASS

Silicates are compounds in which metallic elements combine with silicon and oxygen. Silicates are the largest group of minerals—most rocks contain more than 95% silicates. They are composed largely of silicon and oxygen, with the addition of ions such as aluminum, magnesium, iron, and calcium. The complicated structures that these silicate tetrahedrons form is amazing. They can form as single units, double units, chains, sheets, rings, and framework structures. Structurally, silicates are divided into six classes: (1) neosilicates (single tetrahedrons), (2) sorosilicates (double tetrahedrons), (3) cyclosilicates (rings), (4) inosilicates (single and double chains), (5) phyllosilicates (sheets), and (6) tectosilicates (frameworks). Silicates are usually hard, transparent to translucent, and of average density. Some important rock-forming silicates include the feldspars, quartz, olivines, pyroxenes, amphiboles, garnets, and **micas**.

THE ORGANICS CLASS

The organics class of minerals covers minerals that have an organic chemical component in their formulas. The minerals in this class are created in a geologic setting along with, and beside, nonorganic minerals. They just happen to have organic chemicals in their composition. The organic chemicals, not the minerals, are most likely the result of biological activities, but not always. The minerals are the result of geologic activities and not directly the product of organisms. The minerals of the organics class include the following:

- Amber
- Melanophlogite
- Mellite
- Oxammite
- Wheatleyite
- Whewellite

Amber, or fossilized tree sap, is a beautiful stone that is cut and polished and used as a valuable gemstone. It is also a fossil and can contain many preserved insects and other animals and plants that are tens of millions of years old. The movie *Jurassic Park* (1993) made fossils very well known. The odd inclusions that are often seen in amber usually add to amber's unique look and also increase its value.

Melanophlogite is a very rare mineral found at only a few sites. It forms crystals that appear cubic. Whewellite is the best known of the **crystalline** organic minerals. It is naturally formed as a crystalline solid, with no direct biological connection, and is composed of a set chemical formula. The source of the mineral comes from coal seams and sedimentary nodules and concretions. It has also been found in some hydrothermal veins.

THE MINERALOIDS

The members of this class are often mistaken for minerals and are sometimes classified as minerals, but they lack the necessary crystalline structure to be classified as true minerals. Pearl and jet—two of the better-known mineraloids—are also the products of organic processes. These materials are found naturally; some are treated as gemstones and are included in most mineral references. The mineraloid group consists of the following:

- Jet–very compact coal
- Lechatelierite–nearly pure silica glass
- Limonite–a mixture of oxides
- Obsidian–volcanic silica glass
- Opal–hydrated silica
- Pearl–organically produced carbonate
- Tektites–meteoritic silica glass

In order for all these mineral resources to be useful to humans, there must be a way to mine and process them into useful products, which is addressed in the next chapter.

MINING AND THE DEVELOPMENT OF MINERAL RESOURCES

In order to use minerals as a natural resource, geologists and mining engineers need to know where to find the materials by identifying the rocks that contain high enough concentrations of useful minerals to be developed in an economically feasible way. An ore is a piece of rock that contains enough of an element to make it worthwhile to mine and process. Just because a mineral is abundant does not mean that it is easy to extract from the rocks in which it occurs. If an element is too difficult or expensive to retrieve, it does not make a realistic mining venture. Many rocks are not suitable for use as sources of elements; only those rocks that have undergone some special natural geologic processes that enrich the rock will prove usable. This is why it is important to identify which ores are economically useful.

Also, in order to develop mineral resources into usable products, it usually takes worldwide cooperation. In today's world, no country is truly self-sufficient; not one single country can produce all the different minerals needed to maintain its own economy and society. According to the Mineral Information Institute, the United States despite its vast resources, has to import the following mineral commodities:

- 100% of the columbium (to produce steel), graphite (as a steel hardener), manganese (for iron and steel production), titanium (to construct airplanes), and arsenic (as a wood preservative)
- 99% of the bauxite needed to produce aluminum
- 80% of the tungsten used in lightbulbs and special steels
- 75% of the chromium needed to produce stainless steel
- 70% of the tin, nickel, and zinc needed for the food and medical industries
- 50% of the petroleum needed to provide energy for fuels and other products.

There are a number of environmental issues associated with mining and minerals extraction. Extracting minerals from the surface of the Earth or below the surface requires moving a lot of earth. Extracting 1 ton of copper, for example, requires moving and processing about 350 tons of ore.

Although individual people or small business can sometimes conduct exploration and mining, most modern-day mines are large enterprises requiring large amounts of money in order to operate. Because of this, large—often multinational—companies and various governments dominate the mining industry.

This chapter discusses the development of mineral resources and the mining and refining procedures that are necessary to make them useful resources.

WHAT MUST HAPPEN TO A MINERAL RESOURCE BEFORE IT BECOMES USEFUL

Mineral and energy resources are the ingredients in nearly all the products we use every day. These resources, however, must go through a number of steps or processes before usable items can be produced. Six major processes are involved in developing mineral resources: exploration, extraction, processing, refining, manufacturing, and marketing.

First, the mineral and energy resources must be located—a step called exploration. Geologists must be well trained in order to locate mineral resources. They explore the Earth to find deposits or wells that can be produced.

The next step is extraction. After the resources are located, they must be removed from the Earth. People build surface or underground mines to extract mineral resources. For example, to obtain oil, holes are drilled deep into the Earth. Mining and drilling are two ways mineral resources are extracted.

Usually, valuable minerals are in ordinary-looking rock when they are removed from the Earth. They are often hidden as tiny particles within the rock. The valuable minerals are removed from the rock and concentrated. This is called processing, which involves crushing, grinding, and milling.

Some minerals have to be smelted and refined before they can be made into useful products. For instance, when oil is pumped from the Earth, it is in crude form. The crude oil is sent to a refinery where it is processed into oils, solvents, fuels, and petrochemicals. Copper ore is removed from the Earth with large amounts of rock. The copper must be extracted and processed in order to make it useful.

After the mineral and energy resources are refined, these raw materials are made into products. Their transformation into consumer products is nearly limitless; diverse products include cars, airplanes, computers, fertilizer, and plastic. This is called manufacturing.

Once the products are made, they are sold or marketed. The mineral and energy resource companies sell the mineral resources to a manufacturer. The manufacturer makes a product and sells it to stores, which then sell the products to the public—a process called marketing.

MINING

Mineral deposits are mined to obtain the raw materials that have become indispensable to modern industrial society. To be profitable, the deposit must be big enough to be mined for many years, it must be easy to work, and it must be close to a means of transportation—railroads or ships are the cheapest means. Mineral deposits are most valuable when they are in a confined area. Even if the deposit is rich and close to the surface, it may still be unprofitable to mine if its value is low. Metals can also fluctuate in value, and so an ore that can be worth mining at one time may not be profitable to mine a few years later due to a collapse in the world prices. Tin, gold, and aluminum are examples of such metals.

Ores can be found in many rocks. If the element is extremely valuable—such as gold and platinum—it may be economically feasible to mine even if there are only a few grams of metal per ton of rock. About 40 metal-containing ores are commonly mined. The most easily smelted, or refined, metals are referred to as ore minerals. The ore minerals, however, are nearly always found intermixed with minerals that have no value. The nonvaluable material is called gangue and is usually the majority of the mined material.

Mining is the extraction of valuable minerals or other geologic materials from the Earth. They are usually extracted from an ore body, vein, or seam (as in a coal layer). Many minerals can be recovered from mining processes, such as iron, diamonds, coal, bauxite (used to make aluminum), rock salt, tin, uranium, precious metals (such as gold), lead, limestone, nickel, and phosphate.

Prospecting

Prospecting is the act of searching for minerals or ore deposits. In the past, prospectors explored vast mountainous and canyon areas, carrying picks, shovels, and gold pans. The early exploration for petroleum required drilling hundreds of holes. Most of the early prospectors had no training—they relied mostly on luck.

Prospectors today rely on training and the study of geology and prospecting technology. They use several different methods. Prospectors research areas near past known mineral deposits, rely heavily on geologic mapping, complete rock assay analysis, drill samples from the ground and analyze them in a laboratory, rely on education, and use practical intuition.

Instruments play a large role in gathering geologic data. They can analyze the natural terrain for variations in gravity, magnetism, electro-magnetism, and other variables associated with geologic formations. Geiger counters and scintillometers are used to determine the amount of **radioactivity**. Ultraviolet lamps may cause certain minerals to give off different colors. With the seismic method of prospecting, explosives are used to create small earthquakes. The resulting shock waves can reveal conditions below the Earth's surface.

Chemistry is also used in prospecting. The presence of certain chemical elements can indicate the presence of a specific mineral. Chemical analysis of rocks and plants may indicate the presence of an underground deposit. For example, elements like arsenic and antimony are associated with gold deposits. Vegetation can also be used as an indicator of the presence of certain minerals. Studying dissolved chemicals in streams and underground water can also help locate mineral deposits.

Types of Mining

Depending on the commodity, mining can be done at the surface or underground. Surface methods include strip mining, hill-and-valley mining, and open-pit mining. Underground mining includes room and pillar mining, long-wall mining, removal as an emulsion, and solution mining.

Surface methods

Surface mining costs less than underground mining. Strip mining is a system used when level beds of minerals lie just below the surface over a large area. Strip mining opens up large areas of ground. Today, the land is reclaimed after use, in a process known as a conservation-oriented technique. In this process, a strip of land is dug down to the mineral level. The overlying waste rock and soil is put to one side and stored for return when the site is reclaimed after mining.

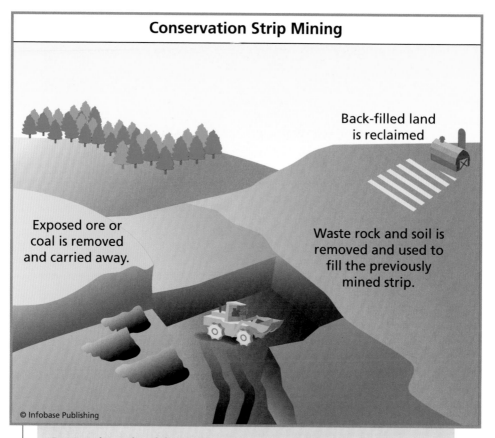

Conservation Strip Mining

Back-filled land
is reclaimed

Exposed ore or
coal is removed
and carried away.

Waste rock and soil is
removed and used to
fill the previously
mined strip.

© Infobase Publishing

Conservation strip mining. As trenches are dug, previously dug trenches are filled in and the land reclaimed.

The mineral is then dug out and the trench widened. As the mining progresses, the trench is refilled; the overburden from the most recent strip fills the strip just mined, in a dig-and-refill sequence. As a result, only a limited amount of overburden has to be placed on the surface of the land at any given time. When the site is finished, the final strip is filled in with the overburden extracted from the first strip, and the topsoil is replaced.

When the landscape is composed of hills and valleys, the mineral is sometimes extracted across the valley side, following the contour of the hill. In this case, the whole top of a hill may be removed gradually, and the fill placed in nearby valleys.

Kennecott copper open-pit mine. Located near Salt Lake City, Utah, it is the largest man-made excavation in the world; and it is even visible to astronauts in outer space. This mine was the birthplace for the concept of open-pit mining. This photo was taken with color infrared film; vegetation appears red, and bare earth is bluish white. The concentric rings that spiral down into the interior of the mine are highly visible; they took decades to dig. *(Courtesy of Nature's Image)*

Where the mineral is contained in a shallow and compact area, mining can be done by digging an open pit. This open pit is never filled in. The pit is dug to leave a series of terraces—called benches—about 49 feet (15 m) high and a spiral ramp for the trucks that have to remove the overburden and mineral.

The pit is enlarged by blasting back into each bench. The ore is drilled and then blasted so that excavators can carry it away. The scale of the equipment that carries away the blasted ore is enormous. For instance, a single scoop can contain 65 cubic yards (50 cubic meters) of

Stone quarries are used to obtain building materials for many items. They are similar to open-pit mines and are mined for sand, gravel, limestone, and other commodities that are used in building materials, such as cement. *(Photo courtesy of Nature's Images)*

material that can weigh more than 100 tons (90 metric tons). The dump trucks used to transport the ore are mammoth—some are the size of a house. This equipment is so big that it is possible to remove half a million tons of material a day. The pit has to slope inward at an angle to ensure that the rock remains stable so the pit does not cave in.

Stone quarrying is similar to open-pit mining. Construction companies often operate quarries. Quarrying is done to collect stone for building and cement, which is made for use in concrete and other building materials. The most useful stones are granite, limestone, sandstone, marble, and **slate**. The **quarry** is normally designed to take special advantage of the natural stone, and so benches vary with the block size of the stone.

Underground mining

Underground mining uses horizontal, sloped, and vertical tunnels to locate and extract the ore. Underground mining must follow the ore vein or coal seam. Following the seam underground can be difficult and costly if the rock is faulted.

Most underground mines have an access shaft that is sunk from the surface down to the many levels that can be worked. Each of the horizontal levels is connected to the shaft by a tunnel called the drift. The shaft contains a cage for carrying both the workers and ore between the different levels. The shafts also contain pipes to pump in air, carry electricity, and pump out water. With underground mining, it is more costly to obtain the ore, so miners attempt to access the ore in the most feasible way possible, while bringing as little waste as necessary to the surface.

One common method of underground mining is called the room-and-pillar method, which keeps the shaft from collapsing underground and trapping the miners. In this procedure, a system of pillars is left unmined. These undisturbed pillars are what hold up the ceiling. Another underground method is called longwall mining. In this procedure, a long wall is established for mining, using an access tunnel at each end. The wall is then mined, and the roof is held up by mechanical jacks. As the long wall is mined out, the jacks are removed, allowing the roof behind to collapse in a controlled way. When the rocks are hard, mining has to be done with pneumatic drills and blasting.

Some minerals are insoluble and can be removed as an emulsion, which is a mixture of water and tiny particles of material. This process operates on the fact that the mineral has a low melting point, but is insoluble. Superheated water at 329°F (165°C) is pumped underground through a pipe, which melts the mineral. Because the mineral is insoluble, it remains chemically uncombined. Inside the main pipe are two smaller pipes. Compressed air is pumped down a central pipe, and a mixture of the liquid mineral, water, and air is pushed up through the

Underground Mine Shaft

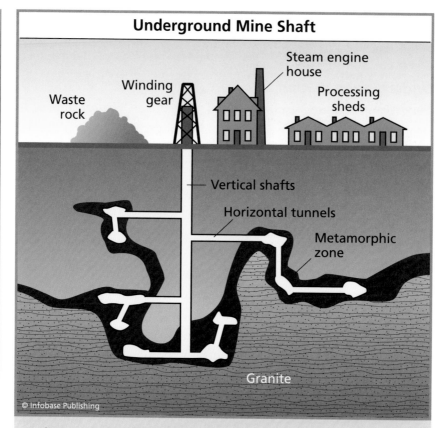

Underground mine shaft schematic. Underground mines can have a series of horizontal, vertical, and sloping tunnels. The tunnels must intersect with the ore body so that the ore can be excavated and delivered to the surface.

remaining pipe. This is called the Frasch process, named after its inventor Herman Frasch, an American chemist, in 1891.

Brine-solution mining is another method of underground recovery of minerals. In particular, salt, potash, and trona (sodium carbonate) are all soluble and so can be removed in solution. A well is sunk to the mineral bed. It is lined (cased), and pipes are inserted into the well. Water is then injected into the well through part of the tube system. Because the brine is denser than the freshwater, it sinks to the bottom. The brine is then sucked up through another part of the tube system. The areas where the solution is extracted can be huge, up to 328 feet

Underground coal mine. The predominant underground mining method in the United States is the *room and pillar method*, a term derived from the mining pattern of a series of excavated areas (rooms) and unexcavated areas (pillars) that are left to support the roof. A major increase in production and efficiency can be achieved by integrating the roof support and extraction function. *(Courtesy of U.S. Department of Energy)*

(100 m) across. When the brine reaches the surface, the water is evaporated away using special vacuum flasks.

Mining Processes

Specific mining processes must occur in order to obtain mineral resources. They must be extracted from the Earth, processed and refined, and then transformed into finished products.

Extraction

Metals are extracted from their ores using chemical reactions. In a reaction to extract metal from its ore, the ore serves as one of the reactants, and the metal becomes one of the products. The higher in the reactivity series the metal is, the more difficult it is to extract from its ore. Because

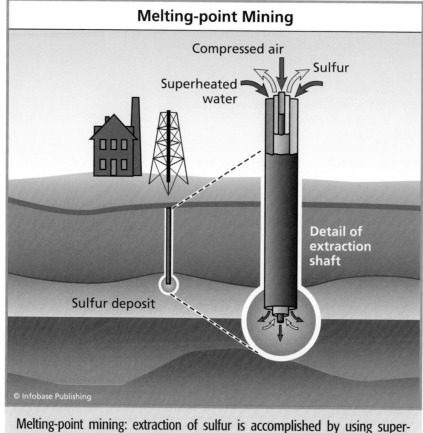

Melting-point Mining

Compressed air

Sulfur

Superheated water

Detail of extraction shaft

Sulfur deposit

© Infobase Publishing

Melting-point mining: extraction of sulfur is accomplished by using superheated water to melt the sulfur so that it can be forced to the surface.

of this, these metals are often more expensive to produce and buy. The main methods of extracting metals from their ores are decomposition, displacement, and electrolysis. All the methods of extracting metals from their ores are also known as smelting.

A decomposition reaction is a reaction in which a compound splits up to make two or more different elements or more simple compounds. Thermal decomposition is decomposition that happens when a material is heated. This type of decomposition works only for metals that are very unreactive. The ores of more reactive metals—such as iron and copper—would have to be heated to an extremely high temperature in order to make them decompose.

When a reactive metal reacts with a less-reactive metal, the more reactive metal displaces the less-reactive metal from the compound. The more-reactive metal forms a new compound, and the less-reactive metal is left as it is. These types of reactions are called displacement reactions.

Electrolysis is a way of splitting a compound into its elements by using electricity. This method decomposes ores that would need to be heated to extremely high temperatures before they would decompose. Aluminum is extracted from its ore by electrolysis.

In the processing phase, either mechanical or chemical processes can be used. Mechanical processes include crushing and flotation. Chemical processes include roasting and smelting. Once the mineral has been located and extracted from the ground, it still must go through more phases before it becomes a useful metal.

The first step in processing is to crush the ore into a powder, because particles in powder form are more easily separated than when they are in larger pieces. Crushing and grinding mills are used to complete this process. Once the powder has left the grinding mill, it must then be concentrated. This is done by making use of the properties of the metal ores involved. For instance, iron can be removed from the gangue by using high-powered magnets. Some metals are denser than the gangue, so flowing water is used to separate them by washing the gangue away.

In the flotation method, the powder is placed in a vat along with water and wetting and frothing chemicals. Jets of air are then blown into the container, making the frothing agents bubble. The chemicals in the vat keep the metals from becoming wet. Because they stay dry, they are caught in the air bubbles and lifted to the surface of the vat, where they float and are collected.

Once the ore has been concentrated by crushing and flotation, the final stages of complete separation—roasting, smelting, and refining—can begin. These are chemical processes, not mechanical ones.

Most naturally occurring metal ores exist as compounds. Smelting is the most effective with compounds that contain oxygen. This requirement is accomplished through the process of roasting it in air (the roasting is the process that adds the oxygen). The ore must be heated above its melting point. When the ore melts, it forms two layers—one containing the metal, the other containing the rest (this waste is called slag).

Iron is the most commonly smelted metal. It is smelted in a blast furnace. Some liquid metal ores can be heated, which turns the metal into a vapor. The vapor is then retrieved. For example, when zinc is smelted, the zinc vaporizes and is condensed. Smelting removes almost all of the impurities.

Refining

This final process is what produces the pure metal. Commonly refined materials include metals, petroleum, and silicon.

Electrolysis is one method of refining. If an electric current is passed through the molten material, pure metal will be deposited on one electrode. Refining also releases gold, silver, and other **impurities** from some commodities. This is an added benefit whose value can be utilized by the mining company.

In the solution method, the roasted material can be dissolved in an acid and the metal withdrawn from the liquid. Oxides and sulfates are commonly refined by solution. Alloying is the process of joining different metals. Alloys are often used because they create stronger metals. One of the most-used alloys today is steel. Steel is an alloy of iron and carbon. Hundreds of millions of tons of steel are produced every year for a multitude of different uses, such as in the construction industry.

Petroleum also needs to be refined in order to transform it into useful products. The main process in a petroleum refinery is distillation, which is accomplished in tall towers. The crude oil is heated and put in the lower part of the tower; the lightest portions are the first to boil off. As they rise through the tower, they cool and condense onto different shelves.

The products that do not boil off are collected and sent to be broken down into smaller molecules—a process called cracking. The cracked fractions are then sent back for refining.

Postprocessing

The final phase of creating useful products is postprocessing. The metal made in most production plants is poured into molds to make masses called **ingots**. In a steel plant, the steel is fed into a machine that shapes it into sheets or bars. This is called "continuous casting." Ingots, bars, and sheets of metal are the raw materials for many finished items.

Casting, forging, and rolling are the three main methods of processing metal. In casting, metal is heated until it melts and is then poured into a mold. The inside of the mold has a hole the same shape as the object to be cast. The hole is filled with metal, which then cools, forming the object. In forging, the metal is heated until it glows red hot, but not enough to melt it. When it is heated, it becomes more malleable, which allows it to be pressed or hammered into shape by machines or hand tools. For example, this is the process blacksmiths use to create and shape horseshoes. In rolling, slabs of metal travel through a set of rollers that flatten them into thin sheets, or bend them around into tubes.

MINERAL RESOURCES FROM THE OCEAN

Oceans cover 70% of the Earth's surface, host a vast variety of geologic processes responsible for the formation and concentration of mineral resources, and are the ultimate repository of many materials eroded or dissolved from the land's surface. Oceans contain vast amounts of materials that are major resources for humans. Today, direct extraction of resources is limited to salt; magnesium; placer gold, tin, titanium, and diamonds; and freshwater.

A hydrothermal vent is a geyser on the seafloor. It continuously spews superhot, mineral-rich water that helps support a diverse community of organisms. Although most of the deep sea is sparsely populated, these hot vent sites teem with a fascinating array of life.

The first hydrothermal vent was discovered in 1977. Hydrothermal vents exist in both the Pacific and Atlantic oceans. Most are found at an average depth of about 7,000 feet (2,100 m) in areas of seafloor spreading along the mid-ocean ridge system. The water that issues from hydrothermal vents consists mostly of groundwater that has percolated down into hot regions from the surface, but it also commonly contains some portion of primordial water that originated deep underground and is only now surfacing for the first time on Earth.

As the hot water (which can reach temperatures of more than 700°F (371°C), escapes from the vents and comes in contact with the near-freezing water of the ocean bottom, the metals quickly form out of their solution. This creates particle-rich water called black smokers, which often erupt out of tall chimneys of previously deposited solidified mineral. They spew mostly iron and sulfide, which combine to form iron monosulfide. This compound gives the smoker its black color.

White smokers release water that is cooler than black smokers and often contains compounds of barium, calcium, and silicon (which are white—hence the name). These vent chimneys can grow rapidly—30 feet (9 m) in 18 months. A scientist at the University of Washington has been monitoring the growth of "Godzilla," a vent chimney in the Pacific Ocean off the coast of Oregon. It reached the height of a 15-story building before it toppled. It is now actively rebuilding.

Because so much metal is spewed out of them, hydrothermal vents have been responsible for many of the world's richest ore deposits, like the copper ores mined on the island of Cyprus in the Mediterranean Sea. Many economic geologists believe that active vents—not just the sites of former ones—can be mined for their massive metallic deposits (although their remote locations might make that difficult).

TECHNOLOGY TO HELP GEOLOGISTS AND MINING ENGINEERS

One of the most dramatic changes in the mining industry has been the role that sophisticated three-dimensional mine-planning software packages have had. Initially, relatively simple tasks—like rendering graphic images of drill holes—meant that it became easier for surveyors, geologists, mine planners, mining engineers, and other technical staff to manipulate and visualize data. In recent years, however, the range of integrated mine-planning tools has meant that massively complex models can be built to optimize the extraction and processing of mineral resources.

MINERAL RESOURCES DATA SYSTEM

The Mineral Resources Data System (MRDS) is a computerized storage, retrieval, and display system developed and managed under the support of the U.S. Geological Survey (USGS). MRDS is an international database of mineral site records with related geologic, commodity, and deposit information. New records are continually being added, and existing records are updated or upgraded. There are several users of the MRDS data, including the USGS, other federal agencies, foreign governments, state agencies, universities, industries, and the general public.

MRDS is a worldwide database of metallic and industrial mineral sites, which was started in 1969 by the USGS. Since 1999, data from MRDS and MAS/MILS (a database maintained by the old Bureau of Mines) have been combined into the MRDS format. Mineral information is stored in records in approximately 200 data fields. Each record can comprise a mineral occurrence, prospect, mining district, region, plant, or mine. A numeric record number uniquely identifies each site. The data fields are grouped under principal categories that can be searched and sorted, including location, geology, description of mineral deposit, exploration and development, description of workings, commodity, production, reserves, and resources.

THE USES OF MINERALS

When people wake up in the morning, they switch on a light. Some people brush their teeth, or look in a mirror and put on makeup. They turn on the radio and make breakfast. They may turn on the television to check the weather or traffic; or they may log onto the computer to check their e-mail. They may go to the bus stop to catch a ride into town or warm up their car in the garage. Just about everything people do in a day involves the use of minerals in one way or another. Think of all the common, ordinary items you see each day: water pipes and electric wiring; refrigerator, radio, toaster, lamp, and lightbulb; sheets, towels, and clothing; soap and toothpaste; window, cereal bowl, juice glass, cocoa cup; water faucet, spoon, doorknob—all were made from or with minerals. Minerals are used every day in tens of thousands of items. This chapter will illustrate the multitude of minerals used in several different applications—all of which make our standard of living what it is today.

MINERALS AND YOU

Everything that cannot be grown—that is neither plant nor animal—is a mineral or made from minerals. Almost every area of human activity depends in some way on minerals. Consider construction, industry and manufacturing, transportation, medical technology, science and electronics—they all utilize minerals. The raw materials from the Earth are as important to our survival as food and water.

According to the U.S. Bureau of Mines, humans use minerals in amounts that range from billions of tons of sand and gravel a year to only thousands of pounds of rhenium—a metal used in producing lead-free gasoline. In the United States alone, it takes more than 2 billion tons of minerals each year to maintain our way of life. This equals about 10 tons of minerals for every man, woman, and child. From those minerals, we get the products we need to live and those that make life more comfortable.

Our dependence on minerals begins with the most basic requirement for life—food. Minerals are necessary for many activities involved in putting food on our tables, such as fertilizers made from potash, phosphate rock, sulfur, and nitrogen that all help plants grow. Farmers use metal tractors and other equipment to plant and harvest crops. Agricultural products such as fruit, vegetables, grain, and livestock are shipped to market in trucks, railroad cars, and airplanes—all these vehicles are made of metal. Metal machines and equipment are used to process and package food into containers made from, or with, minerals. When we eat this food, we are supplied with important nutrients and minerals, such as iron, calcium, phosphorus, magnesium, copper, and zinc. We even take vitamins containing minerals to make sure we get enough.

Minerals are the basis of construction. They provide the building blocks for the houses and apartment buildings; for the towns and cities; and for the roads, highways, and bridges that connect them all together. Every type of modern dwelling is built from minerals. Houses, apartment buildings, offices, and factories have walls of brick, stone, and concrete; roofs made from asphalt and gravel; concrete foundations and gypsum wallboard; metal air conditioners, furnaces, and ventilation ducts; and a vast network of copper pipes, wires, and cables that supply them with water, light, and power. Minerals and mineral-based materials used in construction include cement, sand, clay, tile, lime, glass, aluminum, iron and steel, lead, and zinc.

Many of the goods and products we use each day are made from minerals. Stoves, televisions, refrigerators, microwave ovens, washing

Common Household Items From Minerals

Household item	Minerals used
Carpet	Calcium carbonate, limestone
Glass/Ceramics	Silica sand, limestone, talc, lithium, borates, soda ash, feldspar
Linoleum	Calcium carbonate, clay, wollastonite
Toothpaste	Calcium carbonate, limestone, sodium carbonate, fluorite
Countertops	Titanium dioxide, calcium carbonate, aluminum hydrate
Household cleaners	Silica, pumice, diatomite, feldspar, limestone
Kitty litter	Attapulgite, montmorillonite, zeolites, diatomite, pumice, volcanic ash
Potting soil	Vermiculite, perlite, gypsum, zeolites, peat
Paint	Titanium dioxide, kaolin clays, calcium carbonate, mica, talc, silica, wollastonite
Concrete	Limestone, gypsum, iron oxide, clay
Wallboard	Gypsum, clay, perlite, vermiculite, aluminum hydrate, borates
Microwavable container	Talc, calcium carbonate, titanium dioxide, clay
Pots and pans	Aluminum, iron
Television	35 different minerals and metals
Telephone	42 different minerals and metals

(Sources: U.S. Bureau of Mines and Mineral Information Institute)

machines, radios, and dishwashers contain steel, aluminum, and other metals. Aluminum pots and stainless steel kitchen utensils; brass doorknobs and picture frames; plates and bowls made from china clay; metal tools, bolts, screws, and nails; soaps and detergents made from boron, phosphates, and soda ash; toothpaste, aspirin tablets, lipstick, and eye shadow and other cosmetics containing clay are all mineral products.

It does not stop there. Many materials that are not minerals themselves could not be made without them. One example is glass: sand, selenium, silicon, soda ash, and other minerals are used to manufacture it. Producing paper requires the use of minerals like clay, lime, or sodium sulfate. Minerals like titanium, lead, and cadmium provide coloring for paints.

It is minerals that make possible the manufacture of almost every product bought and sold today. Consider the machines used in factories, plants, mills, and refineries. They are made from steel and other metals. In addition, the processes involved in refining petroleum, making steel, and producing textiles, paper, glass, plastics, and fertilizers depend on chemicals made from minerals.

Transportation would not exist without minerals. From the convenience store down the street to space travel to the Moon and beyond, minerals are used to make it happen. Cars, trucks, and buses; trains, subways, and the rails they run on; barges, ships, and the cranes that unload them—all are made from metal.

The advances in electronics and computer technology that made possible the exploration of space and hundreds of other technical achievements would not be possible without minerals. For instance, copper's ability to conduct electricity not only allows us to light and heat buildings, but also it opened the way to a world of machines that can do many different tasks. Medical analysis involving complicated machinery and technology was derived through the inventive use of minerals.

Directly, or indirectly, the electronics and computer industries use almost every mineral mined today. According to the Mineral

Information Institute, it takes 42 different minerals, for example, to make something as seemingly simple as a telephone handset. From aluminum and beryllium to yttrium and zinc—minerals put light, power, communication, information, and entertainment at our fingertips.

Minerals also provide the materials needed for artistic expression. Painters and sculptors use mineral products—pigments, clay, and marble. The photographer and moviemaker would have no art without silver because silver is used to make film. Symphony orchestras, brass bands, and rock superstars all use instruments made from metal; listening to recorded music would be impossible without equipment made of a wide range of minerals.

The instruments of science—from microscopes and supercomputers to test tubes and beakers—all depend on minerals. All exploration: from universal scale to microscopic scale, involves minerals to make the necessary equipment. Scientists believe that, even into the future, our quality of life will be dependent on minerals and the future uses we may find for them.

INDUSTRIAL APPLICATIONS OF MINERALS

Industry worldwide depends heavily on the use of minerals, metals, and elements. Here are just a few of their applications in the processes of producing goods and services:

- Aluminum–Lightweight parts of cars and airplanes, and construction materials.
- Antimony–A hardening alloy for lead (such as storage batteries); used in bearing metal, type metal, solder, collapsible tubes, and foil; sheet and pipes, rubber and textile industry; and glassmaking.
- Barite–Provides white pigment for paint.
- Barium–Oil well drilling mud, paper industry, rubber industry, filler or extender in cloth, deoxidizer for copper, and spark plug alloys.
- Bauxite–Aluminum ore for soft-drink cans and airplanes.

- Beryllium–Nuclear industry, manufacture of light, strong alloys used in aircraft industry, and deoxidizer in bronze metallurgy.
- Calcite–Provides the matrix in cement.
- Chromite–Used to make steel, "chrome" parts for cars and appliances, and manufacture of chromic acid, which is used to tan much of the leather used in making shoes.
- Coal–Used in the generation of electricity, producing heating oils, and chemicals.
- Cobalt–Super alloys for jet engines, chemicals (paint dryers, catalysts, and magnetic coatings), permanent magnets, and chemical carbides for cutting tools.
- Copper–Pipes, wire, manufacture of brass, bronze coins, and wiring in electrical appliances.
- Dolomite–Used as road aggregate and building stone.
- Feldspar–Used to make bonding material for abrasive wheels, cements, tarred roofing materials, and sizing or filler in textiles and paper.
- Fluorite–Produces hydrofluoric acid, electroplating and plastics industries, metallurgical treatment of bauxite to make aluminum, as a flux to remove impurities in open-hearth steel furnaces and in metal smelting, carbon electrodes, emery wheels, electric arc welders, and paint pigment.
- Galena–Lead ore for pipes, manufacture of batteries.
- Graphite–Dry lubricant, batteries.
- Halite–Petroleum, glass, manufacture of sodium hydroxide, soda ash, caustic soda, hydrochloric acid, chlorine, metallic sodium, ceramic glazes, metallurgy, and curing of hides.
- Hematite–Iron ore, used to make steel for cars, machinery, flatware, stainless steel, construction equipment, manufacturing machinery, highway construction, shipbuilding, trains, railroads, magnets,

high-frequency cores, auto parts, as a catalyst, and in polishing compounds.

- Limestone–Concrete used in the construction of everything from homes and sidewalks to bridges and skyscrapers.
- Limonite–Iron ore, yellow pigment for paint.
- Lithium–Used in primary aluminum production, manufacture of lubricants and greases; rocket propellant, silver, solder, and batteries.
- Magnetite–Iron ore, making steel, construction equipment, manufacturing machinery, highway construction, shipbuilding, trains, railroads, powdered iron is used in magnets, high frequency cores, auto parts, and as a catalyst. Black iron oxide is used in polishing compounds.
- Malachite–Used in wiring to carry electricity to homes, automobiles, and electronic equipment.
- Manganese–Used in steel alloys to increase strength, hardness, and durability (steel cannot be produced without manganese); used as an important colorant to glass (purple amethyst color); manganese nodules on ocean floor may one day be economical.
- Marble–Used as stone in building construction and making decorative items such as pillars, floor and bath tiles.
- Molybdenite–Alloyed with steel and other metals to improve hardness, strength, and resistance to abrasion and corrosion. Used in the manufacture of jet engines, in oil refining, in lubricants, and as pigmentation in dyes, inks, and paint. Used as filament supports in light bulbs because of its high melting point (4,730°F/2,607°C) in metalworking dies and furnace parts.
- Platinum–Used in catalytic converters for the control of automobile and industrial plant emissions, used in catalysts to produce acids, bushings for making glass fibers

used in fiber-reinforced plastic, in electrical contacts, in capacitors, and in resistive films used in electronic circuits.

- Pyrite–Sulfuric acid, manufacture of sulfur, and sulfur dioxide; pellets of pressed pyrite dust are used in the recovery process of iron, gold, copper, cobalt, and nickel.
- Silica–Used to produce glass and refractory materials, ceramics, abrasives, and water filtration processes, as a component of hydraulic cements, as a flattening agent in paints, and as a thermal insulator; used as a filler in the making of paper.
- Silver–Lining of vats and other equipment for use as chemical reaction vessels and in water distillation processes; used as a catalyst in the manufacture of ethylene and in making mirrors.
- Soda Ash–Manufacture of glass containers, fiberglass, specialty glass, and flat glass; used in the papermaking process.
- Sulfur–Sulfuric acid (cleaner), vulcanization of rubber, papermaking.
- Talc–Paints.
- Titanium–Because it is lightweight, strong, and heat resistant, it is used in the manufacture of jet engines, aircraft frames, and space and missile components.
- Trona–Used in the treatment of water for domestic use and the manufacture of chemicals.
- Tungsten–Because of its hardness, it is used in the manufacture of steel (for making tungsten-steel alloys), metalworking, construction. Also used in transportation equipment; for filaments in light bulbs; as components in dyes, enamels, and paints; and for coloring glass.
- Zinc–Protective coating on steel used to manufacture things such as automobile frames and bumpers to prevent corrosion and oxidation (rusting). Used as an alloy metal with copper to make brass, and for "galvanizing" iron used

Many of the standard products used in homes each day originated from minerals, metals, or elements, such as these common household cleaning supplies that you might find under your bathroom sink. *(Photo courtesy of Nature's Images)*

in making nails and roofing material that will not corrode when exposed to the weather.

SCIENCE AND TECHNOLOGY APPLICATIONS

Scientific and technological advancements have never been as fast as they are today; and minerals, metals, and elements have made them all possible. Every time a computer or calculator is used to solve a problem; a watch is looked at; a television, radio, or stereo is turned on for entertainment; an appliance—such as an oven, microwave, stove, dishwasher, can opener, blender, or barbeque grill—is used to accomplish a task; a weather report is received via satellite; a geographical position

Buildings from minerals. Minerals compose nearly all construction items. For example, these buildings are composed of cement (mineral aggregates), marble (for decoration), glass (from quartz), steel beams for framing, cement for sidewalks, metal for street signs, lampposts, metal for hand railings, light bulbs for street lights and interior lights, metal for staircases and elevators, and many other applications. Streets are composed of aggregate, cement, or asphalt. *(Photo courtesy of Nature's Images)*

is calculated using a Global Positioning System (GPS); a military missile is launched; or a rocket is sent into outer space—minerals made that possible. The following list represents just a few of all the many minerals involved:

- Beryllium–A component of the salts used in fluorescent lamps.
- Gold–Provides intricate circuitry and scientific and electronic instruments such as computers.

- Halite–Used in the optical parts of scientific equipment, spectroscopy, ultraviolet and infrared transmissions.
- Silica–Used in televisions and the manufacture of computer chips.
- Silver–Used in telephones, cameras, chemistry, electronics, and scientific equipment.
- Titanium–Used in space and missile components.
- Tungsten–Used in electrical equipment, transportation equipment.
- Quartz–Used in computers, radios, watch batteries, and electronics.
- Vanadium–Used as metal alloys for aerospace applications.

MEDICAL APPLICATIONS

Minerals, metals, and elements affect everyone's health—sometimes in obvious ways, sometimes in not-so-obvious ways. For example, minerals are involved each time someone brushes their teeth, gets an X-ray at a hospital, receives an eye exam, needs a cast for a broken arm, takes an antacid for an upset stomach, or fills a prescription. In fact, without minerals, many things in the medical field would not be possible, and life expectancies would be much shorter than they are today. A few of the minerals involved in the practice of medicine every day are:

- Aluminum–Used in underarm deodorants.
- Antimony–Used in medicines.
- Barite–Used to make barium ore for gastrointestinal X-rays.
- Beryllium–Used in X-ray tubes.
- Calcite–Used in optical equipment.
- Coal–Used in medicines.
- Fluorite–Used in toothpaste, optical equipment.
- Galena (iron)–Used for X-ray shielding.
- Gypsum–Used to produce plaster of Paris (what arm and leg casts are made out of).

- Hematite–Used as a tracer element in biochemical research, medicines.
- Kaolinite–A whitener and abrasive in toothpaste.
- Limestone–Primary ingredient in antiacid tablets and liquids.
- Lithium–Vitamin A synthesis, medicine.
- Magnetite–Radioactive iron used in medicine and as a tracer element in biochemical and metallurgical research.
- Platinum–Used in organic chemicals and pharmaceuticals; dental alloys for making crowns and bridges.
- Potash–Used in medicines.
- Quartz–Used to make optical equipment.
- Silver–Used to make dental and medical equipment.
- Soda ash–Medicines.
- Sulfur–Medicines (sulfa drugs).
- Talc–Talcum powder.

FOOD COMMODITIES AND AGRICULTURAL APPLICATIONS

Minerals also appear in the production of agriculture and processed food items, such as food preservatives, soft drinks, dietary supplements, key food ingredients, and even in the soil from which crops are grown. The following list represents some of the contributions by minerals in these areas:

- Halite–Serves as table salt, flavoring, food preservative, mineral water, animal dietary supplement.
- Manganese–Used as a dietary supplement.
- Phosphate–Phosphoric acid is used in soft drinks to provide the "tingly" taste, used to produce phosphoric acid for ammoniated phosphate fertilizers, feed additives for livestock, elemental phosphorus, and a variety of phosphate chemicals.
- Potash–Used as a fertilizer.

- Silica–Used as an additive to powdered milk, chocolate, and sweeteners.
- Titanium–Used as a whitener in sugar and candy.
- Trona–Used in baking soda and baking powder (a necessary ingredient in making bread, cookies, cakes, and most baked goods).

SUMMARY

From household items, to industrial applications, to science and technology, to medical applications, to food production—minerals are everywhere. If you think about what you do each day, the products you use, and the things you do for entertainment—if you look closely you will be amazed at how many minerals are in your life. The next time you fill your car with gasoline, plan a vacation, go to the dentist for a filling, or to the doctor for a medical procedure or a prescription, thank the existence of the Earth's minerals and the human ingenuity it took to discover, develop, and use them. It is a fact that we would not have the standard of living we enjoy today without the contribution of minerals.

THE IMPORTANCE OF MINERALS

This chapter will focus on some of the other goods and services that minerals, metals, and elements supply—both tangible and intangible. It will look at the way archaeologists, geologists, and paleontologists use the Earth's natural elements to obtain reliable dates for ancient objects—a scientific process called radioactive decay; the employment opportunities and community support made available from major mining corporations; the role minerals play in cultural enrichment, architecture, jewelry, and art; and finally, the critical role that minerals play each day to ensure good human health.

USING ELEMENTS TO DATE ANCIENT OBJECTS— RADIOACTIVE DECAY

In order to determine the age of a rock, assumptions must be made based on its chemical and mineral composition. Geologists are able to examine a rock, measure its composition, and the ratio of various elements. Sometimes, however, these general assumptions may not be correct. The most reliable means of dating an object is through historical evidence. With historical evidence only going back a limited number of years, however, scientists must rely on mineral compositions and radioactive measurements to attempt to date an object.

Scientists know that naturally occurring radioactive materials break down into other materials at known rates. This is referred to as *radioactive decay*. In this process, radioactive *parent* elements decay to stable *daughter* elements.

Radioactivity was discovered in 1896 by Henri Becquerel. In 1905, Ernest Rutherford and Bertram Boltwood first used the principal of radioactive decay to measure the age of rocks and minerals. This is considered to be an outstanding achievement because this was accomplished before isotopes were known and before the decay rates were known accurately. An isotope is any of two or more species of atoms of a chemical element with the same **atomic number** and nearly identical chemical behavior but with differing atomic mass or mass number and different physical properties. The invention of the mass spectrometer after World War I (post-1918) led to the discovery of more than 200 isotopes.

Important Radioactive Isotopes

Radioactive Parent	Stable Daughter	Half-life
Carbon 14	Nitrogen 14	5,730 years
Potassium 40	Argon 40	1.25 billion years
Rubidium 87	Strontium 87	48.8 billion years
Thorium 232	Lead 208	14 billion years
Uranium 235	Lead 207	704 million years
Uranium 238	Lead 206	4.47 billion years

Many radioactive elements can be used as geologic clocks. Each radioactive element decays at its own nearly constant rate. Once this rate is known, geologists can estimate the length of time over which decay has been occurring by measuring the amount of radioactive parent elements and the amount of stable daughter elements.

The table on page 96 illustrates various radioactive parent isotopes and their stable daughter products. The number following the element represents the mass number—the total number of protons plus neutrons. Each radioactive isotope has its own unique half-life. A half-life is the time it takes for half of the parent radioactive element to decay to a daughter product. The table also illustrates the half-lives in years associated with radioactive elements.

Radioactive decay occurs at a constant exponential or geometric rate. The rate of decay is proportional to the number of parent atoms present.

The proportion of parent to daughter tells scientists the number of half-lives, which can be used to find the age of the substance in years. For example, if there are equal amounts of parent and daughter then one half-life has passed. If there is three times as much daughter as parent, then two half-lives have passed.

Radioactive decay occurs by releasing particles and energy. Most minerals that contain radioactive isotopes are in igneous rocks. The dates they give indicate the time the magma cooled. Radioactive elements become concentrated in the residual melt that forms during the **crystallization** of igneous rocks.

Radioactive isotopes do not reveal much about the age of sedimentary rocks or fossils. The radioactive materials in sedimentary rocks are derived from the weathering of igneous rocks. If the sedimentary rocks were dated, the age date would be the time of cooling of the magma that formed the igneous rock. The date would not, however, tell anything about when the sedimentary rock was actually formed.

In order to date a sedimentary rock, it is necessary to isolate a few unusual minerals, if present, which formed on the seafloor as the rock was cemented. Glauconite is an example of this—it contains potassium, so it can be dated using the potassium-argon technique.

There are three methods used in radiometric dating: (1) uranium-lead (U-Pb) dating; (2) potassium-argon (K-Ar) dating, and (3) radiocarbon dating.

Uranium-lead (U-Pb) dating is used primarily on igneous rocks and is used to date objects thought to be very old. Uranium-238 (U-238) has a half-life of 4.5 billion years. In other words, after 4.5 billion years' time, half of the U-238 would have decayed to lead-206. This method makes three assumptions: (1) there is a constant decay rate, (2) there is no loss or gain of uranium or lead during the life of the rock, and (3) it is assumed that no lead existed in the specimen when it was formed.

Potassium-argon (K-Ar) dating is used to date igneous and volcanic rocks. When a rock melts, all the argon-40 gas escapes the lava and enters the atmosphere. From that point on, K-40 decays and forms new Ar-40. The ratio of K-40 to Ar-40 can then be measured and an estimate drawn as to how long ago the rock was molten. This dating method is used on extremely old rocks.

Radiocarbon dating is the third technique. Normal carbon has a molecular weight of 12 (C-12). Radiometric carbon has a molecular weight of 14 (C-14). C-14 is formed in the Earth's atmosphere when ionizing radiation strikes nitrogen-14 and converts it to C-14, which then combines with oxygen to form radioactive carbon dioxide. Living things are in equilibrium with the atmosphere, and the radioactive carbon dioxide is absorbed and used by plants. The radioactive carbon dioxide gets into the food chain and the carbon cycle. All living things contain a constant ratio of carbon-14 to carbon-12. At death, carbon-14 exchanges cease and any carbon-14 in the tissues of the organism begins to decay to nitrogen-14, and is not replenished by new C-14. It is this change in the carbon-14 to carbon-12 ratio that is the basis for dating. The half-life is so short that this method can only be used on materials younger than 50,000 years. Archaeological dating uses this method, as well as dating the ice ages of the Pleistocene epoch. This dating technique assumes that the atmospheric C-14/C-12 ratio is known in the past, or that it is stable.

EMPLOYMENT AND COMMUNITY ENRICHMENT

Large mining operations provide many goods and services to the community. Each operation often employs more than 1,000 people, teaching employees new skills and professions. The operations can also be involved directly with the community by providing financial assistance to schools and educational programs, constructing public buildings, and donating time and money toward assistance to nonprofit organizations and charities. This section will look at one mine in particular as a leading example of what mining can do for a community—the Kennecott Utah Copper Mine, which is a subsidiary of Rio Tinto, one of the largest mining enterprises in the world.

Kennecott is the world's largest man-made feature on the Earth and is the birthplace of open-pit copper mining. Kennecott is located 20 miles (32 km) southwest of Salt Lake City, Utah, in the Oquirrh Mountain range. The name *Oquirrh* is a Ute Indian word meaning "shining mountain." Perhaps it was the massive body of copper ore hidden within the mountain that prompted its Native American name.

In 1906, Daniel Jackling started Utah Copper and established the techniques known as open-pit mining. The original Utah Copper Company was formed in 1903, and in 1906 the first steam shovels came to Bingham Canyon and began stripping waste rock from the sides of a mountain to reach deposits of low-grade copper ore. Small rail cars were used to haul ore through tunnels from Bingham Canyon's underground mines in the late 1800s and early 1900s. That was the beginning of what has become the largest man-made excavation on Earth. The huge open pit mine today is three-quarters of a mile deep (3,960 feet or 1,207 m). For comparison, if the Eiffel Tower in Paris, France, was placed in the bottom of the pit, it would only reach one-third of the way up. If the Empire State Building was put on the bottom of the pit, it would only reach halfway up. The open pit stretches 2.5 miles (4 km) from the widest points at its top.

In the mining process, drilling and blasting is a critical part of the process of obtaining the ore. Drill rigs bore (drill) a series of holes 55 feet (17 m) into the bench levels of the mine. Each blast hole is then

The Kennecott mine in Bingham Canyon, Salt Lake County, Utah, is the world's largest open-pit copper mine. *(Courtesy of Nature's Images)*

A hauler at the Kennecott copper mine is roughly the size of a small house. *(Courtesy of Nature's Images)*

The tires used on the ore haulers are enormous. A steel-belted radial tubeless tire: each one measures 12.5 feet (3.8 m) in height, has a diameter of 153 inches (389 cm), weighs 10,183 pounds (4,619 kg), has a tread width of 55 inches (140 cm), and has a rim size of 63 inches (160 cm). Each tire lasts about one year (50,000 miles (80,467 km)) and costs $25,000. The haulers have six tires on them at a cost of $150,000 per year for each truck. *(Photo courtesy of Nature's Images)*

loaded with 1,000 pounds (454 kg) of special explosives. Two to four times a day, the explosives are detonated to break up the rock for the mining operations.

Mining the ore, using huge electric shovels and king-sized haulage trucks, is just the first step in the production of copper. The metal-bearing ore, which contains less than 1% copper, is delivered to the in-pit crusher. The rock is loaded onto a conveyor that travels 3 miles (4.8 km) through a tunnel in the mountain to the Copperton Concentrator. Ore is crushed to about the size of soccer balls. The in-pit crusher reduces the ore to about 10 inches (25.4 cm) and deposits it onto a 5-mile (8 km) conveyor.

The crushed ore is then mixed with water and ground to a powder. Through a flotation process, the ore is "concentrated" to 28% copper by removing unwanted materials. In the process, a valuable by-product, molybdenum, is recovered and sold to steel manufacturers as a hardening agent. The concentrated ore, mixed with water, is pumped 17 miles (27 km) through a pipeline to the smelter near the Great Salt Lake.

The 28% copper concentrate is heated to a molten state and additional impurities (primarily iron and sulfur) are removed in a revolutionary flash smelting and converting process. The molten copper, 99.5% pure, is poured into forms called anodes, then cooled and shipped to the nearby electrolytic refinery.

Anodes are subjected to an electrolytic process where the copper is refined to a purity of 99.99%. During the process, precious metals, such as gold and silver, are also recovered as by-products. The finished copper cathodes are then shipped to manufacturers that produce a broad range of industrial, aviation, military, and construction products, as well as other copper, brass, and bronze consumer products we all use every day.

Annually, Kennecott produces 300,000 tons (272,155 metric tons) of copper—which represents 17% of the total U.S. copper output. They have the safest and most efficient processes in the world. They also strive to be the cleanest. They have specially designed furnaces that completely control the wastes and emissions. The waste sulfur is sold to farmers as fertilizer, adding another economic benefit to the community.

Kennecott is also concerned about environmental quality and have an established track record to support it. They have spent $350 million in environmental improvements, including planting more than 150,000 trees and thousands of acres of bushes, flowers, and grass. Supporting an environmentally sound approach to mining, they have cleaned up and reclaimed old mine sites that were operated prior to the formation of Kennecott. They have reclaimed their older tailings; engineers and scientists control air emissions, monitor and improve water quality, and recycle 300,000 gallons (1,135,624 liters) per minute of water; and they provide homes to many species of wildlife, such as deer, fox, mountain lion, elk, and host one of the largest inland seashore bird refuges in North America. They even lease land to the U.S. Bureau of Land Management to provide a home for the wild horses and burros brought in under the Adopt-a-Horse Program.

In addition, 99.9% of the sulfur given off in the various processes is captured as waste heat, which is then used to generate 60% of their own internal power needs. Kennecott has spent $2 billion to modernize over the last 10 years in order to make the processes cleaner and more efficient.

All these operations that are involved in mining and refining copper serve the community by providing employment opportunities to many people. Currently, Kennecott has about 1,300 employees on their payroll, providing significant support to the local and national economies.

Kennecott also serves the community in other ways. Every year, they contribute to hundreds of local charities, civic and arts organizations, as well as schools, colleges, and universities. They also sponsor a program exclusively for public welfare, community improvement, and charitable purposes, which provide help to the poor and needy, with an emphasis on the disabled, children, and the elderly.

Kennecott sponsors a nature center along the Jordan River, providing homes to many different species, such as great blue herons, mallards, and foxes. They host an educational program, which benefits many of the schools in the community. In addition to their contributions to charities, education, and the arts, they look for one or two larger projects each year that will leave a lasting legacy in the community. The Kennecott Nature Center was one of these projects. Their involvement benefits other communities as well. For example, they are currently involved in reclaiming and cleaning up many mining sites located throughout the United States, such as in Nevada, Wyoming, and Alaska.

CULTURAL ENRICHMENT

Many cultures worldwide incorporate minerals into their beliefs. One example is the Native-American culture of North American tribes; in particular, the Zuni tribe of the Southwest and their use of fetishes (small animal stone carvings). Traditional Native-American culture holds that all things have a spirit. They believe animals have more power than humans and that these powers reside in fetishes.

The Zuni use fetishes for many purposes—carvings from different minerals have specific meanings. In general, for Native-American tribes, fetishes are believed to offer powerful aid in hunting, diagnosing and curing disease, mediating between gods and emissaries, initiation of war, farming, weather control, fire-making, propagation and fertility, defense against witchcraft, and punishment. They are believed to protect individual owners or entire communities (regarding rain and bountiful harvests).

The intrigue of fetishes has also spread to other cultures. Today, according to the *Wall Street Journal*, a growing number of mainstream business executives and professionals buy and use Native-American fetish carvings for career success. For example, one attorney claims that her bear fetish helps her balance aggression and patience in the courtroom. A professional photographer uses the buffalo fetish as a symbol of abundance, hoping to land many projects. A computer software executive takes an eagle fetish to trade shows to help him receive greater insight into what is going on. Many people use fetishes as spiritual guides. Fetishes can be carved from a variety of rocks and minerals, such as agate, fluorite, amber, basalt, onyx, hematite, sandstone, gypsum, turquoise, and many others.

These Native-American fetishes are carved from many different minerals. The outside of the pot is adorned with crushed turquoise—a sacred stone to many tribes. Each mineral and animal type has special meaning in its culture. *(Courtesy of Nature's Images)*

Many fetishes have so-called medicine bundles on their backs—consisting of arrowheads, stones, and shells—which are believed to add increased power for the fetish or to express gratitude for blessings received or anticipated.

Many serious fetish owners provide a fetish jar for their collection. Because fetishes are said to house the living spirit of the animal they represent, they must be cared for and fed as a living creature to ensure their power. The fetish pot in the photo above is covered with crushed turquoise—a sacred mineral to the Native Americans. Crushed corn-meal is placed inside to offer nourishment.

Other cultures have also incorporated minerals into their traditions. Crystals, minerals, and metals have played various roles in the myths and legends of human cultures throughout history—such as with the Greeks, Romans, and Egyptians. They are fascinating examples of the attempts of various cultures to explain their world without the benefit of modern science and its fields such as astronomy, meteorology, geology, oceanography, and chemistry. Archaeologists have used past evidence of these beliefs to better understand the psychology of ancient peoples. Today, some people believe quartz has the power to heal and carnelian gives its owner better self-esteem.

MINERALS IN ARCHITECTURE

Many beautiful buildings have been created throughout the ages through the use of rocks and minerals. Granite and marble are common building materials. These materials are not only durable and resist weathering, but they provide highly workable materials for large-scale construction. The Eiffel Tower in Paris, France, is comprised of steel—a network of girders supports its nearly thousand-foot height.

Granite is a stone that is frequently used to obtain beautiful and stunning architecture. The building in the photos on pages 107–108 illustrates the beauty of granite as a building material. Because it can be readily cut, carved, and shaped, it is possible for master craftsmen to achieve stunning detail in buildings that will last for centuries.

JEWELRY AND ART

Throughout the world, various cultures have established styles or types of jewelry that are unique to their geographical regions. These culturally unique designs arise from a combination of the background of the people in the area and what local natural resources are available to them to make jewelry.

Jewelry consisting of metals like gold, silver, platinum, and copper are valued in most areas of the world. At various times in history, silver has been valued even more than gold. It has also had a mystical allure to it, often being associated with the sea and the Moon. Hallmarking is

Beautiful buildings can be crafted from stone, such as granite. This is a temple in Salt Lake City, Utah (the Church of Jesus Christ of Latter-day Saints). The granite was hand-excavated and hauled 25 miles (40 km) to the construction site in the 1800s. It took 40 years to construct. The building's outer structure is composed entirely of granite. The gold in the statue on the top and the gold inlay on the wall are gold leaf. The statues in the foreground are made of bronze. The building on the left side of the photo is also made of granite and intricately carved. *(Photo courtesy of Nature's Images)*

This is the same building as shown on page 107. Notice the intricately carved decorations on the granite walls—the stars, spires, and scallops make this building look like a castle. Many view architectural carving in granite as an artistic skill. *(Photo courtesy of Nature's Images)*

Gold has always been valued in the making of jewelry, as are various gemstones. This collection shows a solid gold watch and gold ingot, as well as rings that have been set with diamond, ruby, emerald, opal, topaz, sapphire, alexandrite, and Black Hills gold. *(Courtesy of Nature's Images)*

where a stamped mark is placed on the silver to identify its origin and purity. This is often an important part of determining the value of a collectable piece.

Sterling silver is composed of 92.5% silver alloyed with copper to strengthen it. It has one of the highest reflectivities of any metal, giving it unmatched brilliance and making it very popular for jewelry designs. Silver is also relatively abundant and easy to extract from ore, so it is affordable, which makes it an ideal metal for jewelry. There are other alloys of silver with a higher silver content than sterling. Mexican and Brittania silver each have about 95% silver. Coin silver, on the other hand, typically has 90% or less silver content.

The Hope Diamond is one of the world's most famous diamonds. At 45.52 carats, it is the largest in the world. Its deep blue color is due to trace amounts of boron in the stone. *(Photo courtesy of Calvin Hamilton, ScienceViews)*

Many cultures have designated different gemstones to correspond with different months to create birthstones. One of the most highly valued and symbolic of these gemstones is diamond. One of the most famous diamonds in the world is the Hope Diamond. At 45.52 carats, it is the world's largest deep blue diamond. It is more than a billion years old, was formed deep within the Earth, and carried by a volcanic eruption to the surface in what is now present-day

India. Since the Hope Diamond was discovered in the early 1600s, it has crossed oceans and continents and passed from kings to commoners. It has been stolen and recovered, sold and resold, cut and recut. Through it all, the diamond's value increased. In 1958, Harry Winston donated the Hope Diamond to the Smithsonian Institution in Washington, D.C., and it now belongs to the people of the United States.

In the pendant surrounding the Hope Diamond (which is blue due to trace amounts of boron in the stone) are 16 white diamonds. The necklace chain contains 45 white diamonds.

Minerals are also popular in art. For centuries, minerals have been used to create different pigments (colors) for use in pottery, ceramics, paints, and dyes. Hematite, yellow ocher, and other natural Earth pigments were used in the Stone-Age paintings on cave walls. The durability over time of these materials is evident in many examples found throughout the world today. As ages passed, other pigments were discovered and incorporated into the art of the time. Many of these early colors were as prized and sought after as rare gems.

Statuary is another popular form of art. Statues are often sculpted of metal such as bronze. One of the most famous and well-known statues worldwide is the Statue of Liberty in New York. The Statue of Liberty is made of copper. Copper and its alloys—bronze (copper and tin) and brass (copper and zinc)—provide warmth and versatility to art objects and hundreds of other decorative uses. History tells us that the ornamental and artistic uses of metal came long before industrial applications. The Statue of Liberty is renowned as the tallest copper statue in the world. It stands 152 feet (46 m) tall and its 200,000-pound (90,718 kg) outer covering is formed of more than 300 hand-shaped sheets of copper only 3/32-inch (0.23 cm) thick. It has been the symbol of U.S. liberty since 1886.

Rocks and minerals are also used indoors as decorative pieces of art and statues. Rocks may be displayed in their raw form, to demonstrate their completely natural beauty, or sculpted into specific forms.

The Statue of Liberty is the world's tallest copper statue. The statue looks green because over time the copper oxidizes with the air, changing its brilliant shine to a dull pale green. *(Photo courtesy of Nature's Images)*

MINERALS FOR HUMAN HEALTH

Just like vitamins, minerals help a body grow, develop, and stay healthy. The human body uses minerals to perform many different functions—from building strong bones to transmitting nerve

Minerals are commonly crafted into pieces of art. Many people decorate with various minerals. This photo illustrates the diversity of beautiful products that can be created from minerals. Beginning at the left, the purple statue is amethyst, cut from a geode; the layered obelisk is sedimentary rock; the large sample on the back right is a cut from a geode; the white bear is composed of ceramic (clay) and ash from the Mount St. Helen's volcanic eruption in 1981; the pirate medallion is a metal alloy; the bear behind it is metal and sandstone; the owl is carved jet; the earrings are silver and various stones; and the clear obelisk is quartz. *(Courtesy of Nature's Images)*

impulses. Some minerals are used to make hormones or maintain a normal heartbeat.

There are two kinds of minerals: essential minerals (also called macro minerals) and trace minerals. Essential minerals are those needed in larger quantities. This group includes magnesium, phosphorus, calcium, sulfur, sodium, chloride, and potassium. Trace minerals are those that are needed only in small amounts. They include iodine, zinc, cobalt, iron, copper, fluoride, manganese, and selenium.

If someone does not receive an adequate amount of these minerals on a regular basis, they can have health problems. A well-known example is calcium. If someone does not get enough calcium, his or her bones can be weak. This can lead to diseases such as osteoporosis.

There are 92 elements found in nature, and an additional 22 theoretical and/or observed elements. In addition, there are hundreds of isotopes of the elements, any one of which may play a future role in good human health. Researchers have found increasing evidence

Food Sources of Minerals

Calcium

Calcium is the top essential mineral when it comes to your bones. This mineral helps build strong bones and teeth. Foods most rich in calcium include:

- Dairy products (milk, cheese, and yogurt)
- Leafy green vegetables (such as broccoli)
- Calcium-fortified foods (orange juice, cereals, and crackers)

Iron

The body needs iron to transport oxygen from the lungs to the rest of the body. It is also important in the formation of hemoglobin, which is the part of your red blood cells that carries oxygen throughout the body. Iron-rich foods include the following:

- Red meat
- Tuna
- Salmon
- Eggs
- Beans
- Baked potato with skins
- Raisins
- Leafy green vegetables, such as broccoli
- Whole and enriched grains (wheat or oats)

when studying the relationship of minerals to human health that keeping the level of minerals in balance in every tissue, fluid, cell, and organ in the human body may be the key to maintaining long-term good health.

Essential minerals perform many vital bodily functions and processes. The two most abundant minerals in the body are calcium and phosphorus. Calcium can be found in the teeth and bones; and phosphorus can be found in the teeth, bones, and muscles.

Potassium

This keeps the muscles and nervous system healthy. It also helps make sure the amount of water in the blood and body tissues is balanced correctly. Foods rich in potassium include the following:

- Broccoli
- Potatoes
- Citrus fruits (lemons, oranges, and grapefruit)
- Legumes (beans, peas, lentils, and peanuts)
- Dried fruits
- Leafy green vegetables
- Tomatoes
- Bananas

Zinc

Zinc helps the immune system to fight off disease. It also promotes cell growth and speeds up the healing process for wounds. Foods that are rich in zinc include the following:

- Beef
- Pork
- Lamb
- Legumes (beans, peas, lentils, and peanuts)

(Source: The Nemours Foundation)

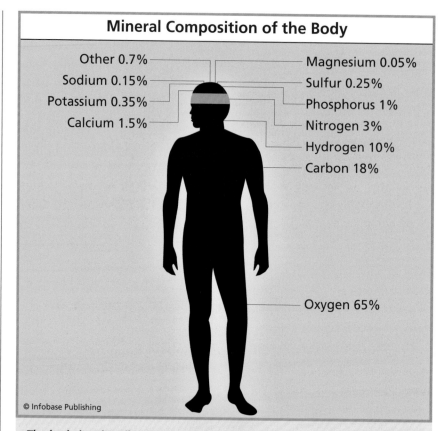

Mineral Composition of the Body

Other 0.7%
Sodium 0.15%
Potassium 0.35%
Calcium 1.5%

Magnesium 0.05%
Sulfur 0.25%
Phosphorus 1%
Nitrogen 3%
Hydrogen 10%
Carbon 18%

Oxygen 65%

© Infobase Publishing

The body is primarily composed of oxygen, carbon, hydrogen, and nitrogen. Other minerals—such as calcium, potassium, and sodium—exist in smaller quantities but are valuable in maintaining good health.

Calcium is required throughout life to keep bones and teeth strong. The calcium in blood has very useful and has important functions to perform, so much so that the body will actually pull calcium from the bones to make sure there is enough in the blood. Calcium in the blood helps regulate heartbeat, controls blood pressure, clots blood, contracts muscles and sends messages along nerves. In addition, calcium is required to make certain hormones and enzymes. It also helps build connective tissues.

Trace minerals also occur naturally in the body but in very tiny amounts (larger amounts of these minerals would be toxic). Although they are necessary in only small amounts, they are very important. Some of the most important minerals include chloride, chromium, copper, iodine, iron, magnesium, manganese, molybdenum, phosphorus, potassium, selenium, silica, sodium, and zinc.

Chloride—along with potassium and sodium—is an electrolyte. An electrolyte is a mineral that dissolves in water and carries an electrical charge. Since the body is mostly made up of water, electrolytes are found everywhere in the body—inside the cells, the spaces between the cells, in the blood, in lymph glands, and everywhere else. Because electrolytes have electrical charges, they can move easily back and forth through membranes. This is important because as they move out of cells, they carry out waste products and excess water. To keep body fluid levels in balance, cells need to have a little potassium inside them and a lot of sodium in the fluids outside them. To keep the balance, sodium and potassium constantly move back and forth through the cell membranes. Chloride in the diet works with potassium and sodium—the two electrolytes—to control the flow of fluid in blood vessels and tissue, as well as regulating acidity in the body. Chloride also forms part of the hydrochloric acid in the stomach.

Chromium is an essential nutrient required for normal sugar and metabolism and works by ensuring insulin acts correctly and is present throughout the entire body, but with the highest concentrations in the liver, kidneys, spleen, and bones. Chromium is needed for energy, as it maintains stable blood sugar levels. It helps control certain enzymes; and is also required in the synthesis of fats, protein, and carbohydrates. Chromium is only needed in small amounts, but it has proven to be important in preventing hypoglycemia and diabetes.

Copper is required in the formation of hemoglobin, red blood cells, and bones. It also helps wounds to heal. It is essential for energy production, connective tissue formation, iron metabolism, and also acts as an antioxidant. Copper is also important for the manufacture of the neurotransmitter noradrenaline.

Iodine is required to make the thyroid hormones that regulate metabolism. The thyroid hormones play a big role in growth, cell reproduction, nerve function, and how cells use oxygen. One of the thyroid hormones—thyroxin—regulates how fast the body uses the energy from food.

Iron is required to carry oxygen in the blood. Every one of the red blood cells in the body contains a protein called hemoglobin. In the lungs, oxygen molecules attach to the iron atoms and are carried to the blood cells. When the oxygen reaches its destination, it is swapped for the waste carbon monoxide and carried back to the lungs where it is removed by inhalation.

Every cell in the body needs magnesium to produce energy. It is required to make more than 300 different enzymes and to send messages along the nerves. Magnesium makes the muscles relax, which ensures the heart is healthy. It is also needed to keep blood pressure down to normal levels. Magnesium works very close with calcium to help keep bones strong throughout life.

Manganese plays an important role in a number of physiological processes as a constituent of some enzymes and an activator of other enzymes. Manganese-activated enzymes play important roles in the metabolism of carbohydrates, amino acids, and cholesterol. It enables the body to better use vitamin C and vitamin B1. Manganese is also necessary for healthy bone and cartilage development, as well as wound healing. It assists in preventing diabetes and it is needed for normal nerve function.

Phosphorus is an essential mineral that is required by every cell in the body for normal function. It plays an active role in bone and teeth formation, as well as most metabolic actions in the body. It is also involved in converting food to energy.

Potassium, along with sodium and chloride, is an electrolyte. (Electrolytes are found everywhere in the body.) Because potassium can move back and forth through cell membranes, it is able to carry nutrients in with it and carry out waste products and excess water. Potassium helps keep body fluid levels in balance.

Selenium is another important mineral. It helps fight infections by stimulating increased antibody response. One of the main activities of selenium is its role in antiaging and its ability to help rid the body of dangerous chemicals known as free radicals, as well as toxic minerals such as mercury, lead, and cadmium.

Silica helps keep bones, cartilage, tendons, and artery walls healthy. The nails, hair, and skin also require to stay in good condition.

Zinc is very important for correct functioning of the immune system. Taking extra zinc during a bad cold or flu can help quicken healing. It also helps the body heal quicker from wounds, keeps the skin healthy, and helps preserve eyesight. More than 200 different enzymes in the body depend on zinc to work properly. It is not hard to see why minerals are important to strong bodies and good health.

MANAGEMENT OF MINERAL RESOURCES

Management of mineral resources is important not only for current production, but also for future planning. Mining practices must take into consideration sustainable yield and conscientious stewardship so that future generations will also have minerals available for their use. Mining practices must be efficient as well as cost effective in order to avoid wasted resources and environmental degradation. Management practices must also deal with the presence of abandoned mines—some centuries old—that are causing environmental hazards to the areas surrounding them.

This chapter examines the management of mineral resources. It looks at active mine management and the technology that helps mining engineers and managers operate efficiently; it focuses on hazardous waste management and the serious problems associated with abandoned mines; it looks at mine reclamation, chemical contamination, rehabilitation issues, environmental impact, and wildlife restoration enhancement.

ACTIVE MINING MANAGEMENT

Management of mining operations must be efficient, cost effective, safe, and environmentally sound. Recent technological developments have greatly assisted managers in being able to meet these expectations. Mines today are managed by computers and tools such as Geographic Information Systems (GIS). Today, the use of GIS is gathering momentum in the mining industry as a powerful tool for analyzing and displaying data. Of particular interest is the ability of GIS to link spatial features to tabular data. Graphic data—such as CAD drawings, Global Positioning System (GPS) data, and aerial photography (remote sensing)—can have tables of corresponding data (such as field measurements and lab analysis results) linked to the graphics so that using the visual data along with the tabular data creates a useful management tool.

For example, an application of GIS in underground mining can bring together data from four areas: land ownership and mineral claims, exploration management, production, and mine safety issues. The benefits to consolidating and archiving claims data, and the ability to georeference property maps defined in local coordinates into a more widely used coordinate system, is extremely important to managers so that trespass and other legal issues do not occur. In mine production, GIS facilitates locating areas with the highest likelihood of being not only productive but also mineable and economical. These factors must exist for a successful mining operation. In mine safety, areas of potential safety concerns can be identified through a process called proximity analysis (choosing areas of safe retreat that are closely located to possible hazardous areas). GIS can be used to calculate and map out the shortest routes to emergency exits and enable a workable mine-safety evacuation plan to be put in place. GIS can be used as a three-dimensional tool to map the areas of highest mineral concentration and relate that information to the topography in order to determine the best way in which to mine the resource.

GIS has other applications in mine management, as well. For instance, transportation routes can be identified and mapped. Managers can plan the best routes for transporting goods and supplies from the

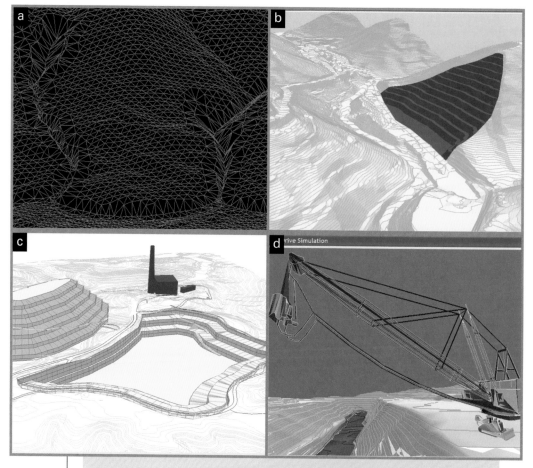

Geographic Information Systems and 3-D modeling are often used in mining applications. Computer models can be developed to locate various concentrations of ores and evaluate the slope of the land. Once the highest concentrations of ore are found, the contours of the land are used to decide where best to start digging. (a) A triangular network is a GIS modeling technique used to depict the subtle changes in surface character of the Earth. (b) By modeling the land's contours, as seen in this mine pit design, the exact placement of the levels of the open pit can be mapped out prior to digging. (c) This drawing illustrates where mining engineers will dig the pit and place the stockpile of removed earth material. (d) Excavating equipment called a dragline helps mining engineers determine how to most efficiently dig the mineral. *(a, courtesy of AERO-METRIC, Inc.; b, c, d, courtesy of Carlson Software)*

nearest community to the mine site. Integrating data such as topography, land ownership, land use, population, and climatic conditions can help in finding the most economical and environmentally responsible mining practices. GIS and remote sensing can assist planners in identifying natural hazards such as potential landslides, earthquakes, floods, and volcanic eruptions prior to the construction of production and housing facilities.

Planners of a new mine may need information on population density, socioeconomic distribution, labor resources, housing, and recreational sites that may potentially be affected by the mining operation. This information is needed to prepare the environmental impact assessment that is required before mining can begin. GIS is a very useful tool for this type of application.

GIS can also aid in the selection of a housing site close to the mining operation that meets safety and other requirements. Topographic, vegetative, drainage, and soil information can be incorporated into a mine management analysis. In today's complex environment, GIS has many applications in the mining industry providing tools to gather, compile, process, display, analyze, and archive vast amounts of data.

HAZARDOUS WASTE MANAGEMENT

Hazardous waste is waste that for one reason or another makes it dangerous or potentially harmful to human health or the environment. There are many types of hazardous waste. For example, waste can be liquids, solids, gases, or sludges. It can be the by-products of manufacturing processes or manufactured commercial products, like cleaning fluids or pesticides. Unfortunately, there are many environmental issues associated with mining and minerals extraction. Extracting minerals from the surface of the Earth or below the surface requires moving a lot of earth. Although reclamation of land disturbed by mining operations is now required by law, some disturbances are permanent. In many mining operations, waste products are generated. These wastes must be managed very carefully so that toxic materials do not leak into the environment and contaminate water, soil, air, or anything else that comes in contact with life forms.

One of the biggest obstacles the United States faces today is addressing the issue of cleaning up old, abandoned mines—mining operations in existence well before the environmental dangers had been realized, studied, and controlled. In many cases, the companies that operated these mines are not around today. This makes it hard to assign liability for the costs of cleaning up the site.

Two materials that pose a problem for waste management are lead and asbestos. Lead is a highly toxic metal that was used for many years in products found in and around homes. Lead may cause a range of health effects, from behavioral problems and learning disabilities to seizures and death. Children six years old and younger are most at risk because their bodies are growing quickly. Researchers suggest that the primary sources of lead exposure for most children are from deteriorating lead-based paint, lead-contaminated dust, and lead-contaminated residential soil.

The U.S. Environmental Protection Agency (EPA) is playing a major role in addressing these residential lead hazards and has had a considerable amount of success. For example, in 2002, about 310,000 children were tested as having elevated blood lead levels in the United States. Two decades earlier, almost 4 million people were diagnosed with unhealthy lead levels. Under the EPA's direction, the amount of lead has been reduced in drinking water and in industrial air pollution. The EPA has also banned (or limited) the amount of lead used in consumer products, such as residential paint. To further address the lead problem, states and communities have set up programs to identify and treat lead-poisoned children and to rehabilitate deteriorated housing. Parents have helped to reduce their children's exposure to lead by cleaning and maintaining their homes, having their children's blood lead levels checked, and promoting proper nutrition.

Asbestos has been in use for centuries and has long been recognized for its useful properties, such as the ability to resist heat and provide beneficial insulating properties. The term *asbestos* describes six naturally occurring fibrous minerals. The three most commonly used are chrysotile (white asbestos), amosite (brown asbestos), and crocidolite (blue asbestos). Chrysotile is used in buildings, amosite is used as a fire retardant in thermal insulation products and ceiling tiles, and crocidolite is used in high-temperature applications.

During the Industrial Revolution in the 1800s, asbestos was used for insulating pipes, boilers, and fireboxes in steam locomotives. Refrigeration units, boxcars, and cabooses were also lined with asbestos insulation. Shipyards were full of asbestos, and shipbuilders used the mineral to insulate steam pipes, boilers, hot-water pipes, and incinerators. The automotive industry also used it—clutch and brake linings usually contained asbestos. In fact, many cars on the road today still contain parts made with asbestos.

The most widespread use of asbestos has been in the building and construction industry. Its insulating and flame-retardant properties made asbestos the perfect material for keeping buildings warm and safe. Not only was asbestos used for insulation in walls but also in such materials as siding; floor and ceiling tiles; roofing tars and shingles; cement pipes, gutters, and rainwater pipes; mud and texture coats like stucco; plaster, putty, and caulk; and even stage curtains in theaters and schools. Asbestos has been used in various products since the 1900s, but the peak usage years were between 1950 and 1975. It was considered an ideal material to use, since it resembles fibers such as cotton and wool in its pliability and softness, yet it is inflammable and acid resistant.

The U.S. Geological Survey estimates that, in all, as many as 3,000 products may, at one time or another, have contained asbestos, including a number of household items that would otherwise seem harmless, such as handheld hair dryers, coffee pots, toasters, irons, ironing board covers, electric blankets, and burner pads.

This is not just a modern day problem, however. The recognition of the dangerous properties of asbestos goes back to the Roman Empire when concerned citizens and doctors noticed that those who worked in asbestos mines were dying early or developing lung-related diseases. Records show that by the turn of the twentieth century, insurance companies were already charging higher premiums or refusing coverage to those who had jobs that exposed them to asbestos.

It was not until the 1970s that government agencies, such as the EPA and the Occupational Safety and Health Administration (OSHA) began to regulate asbestos and its uses. By that time, many people had been exposed to asbestos and asbestos-containing products for a number of years. Cleanup of asbestos still continues today, usually when buildings are remodeled. Presently, the United States generally does not use asbestos in the manufacture of products due to health concerns and liability issues. However, other countries do not have strict controls in place against it and so imported materials may still contain asbestos.

RECLAMATION ISSUES

For many years, the mining industry was not heavily regulated. In fact, mines could be prospected, worked, depleted, and abandoned without the owner facing any regulations or environmental responsibilities of any kind. When the problems related to this began to surface, regulations began to be put into place.

U.S. Mining Laws

The General Mining Act of 1872 is a U.S. federal law that authorizes and governs prospecting and mining for economic minerals, such as gold and silver, on public-owned lands. Today, the acquisition of mining rights on public land in the West is mostly governed by the 1872 Act, although there have been some amendments made to the Act since its inception. These amendments cover nonmetallic minerals; sale of certain minerals, such as sand and gravel; and the development of multiple minerals on the same tracts of public lands. Many conservation groups, however, feel this law has become antiquated and that there are not enough regulations imposed on the mining industry.

In 1977, the Surface Mining Control and Reclamation Act (SMCRA) was signed into law. This is the principal federal law that regulates the environmental effects due to mining processes. It has two main parts: (1) regulation of active mines, and (2) reclamation of abandoned mines. SMCRA also created the Office of Surface Mining, an agency within the U.S. Department of the Interior, to oversee regulations, fund state regulatory and reclamation efforts, and make sure the regulations between states are consistent.

These regulations set environmental standards that mines must follow while operating and goals they must meet when reclaiming mined land. SMCRA requires that companies obtain permits before conducting surface mining. They must describe (1) what the premining environmental conditions and land use are, (2) what the proposed mining and reclamation will be, (3) how the mine will meet the standards, and (4) how the land will be used after reclamation is complete. SMCRA also prohibits mining to be conducted in sensitive areas, such as national parks and designated wilderness areas.

Also created under this Act were provisions concerning abandoned mine land (AML), a huge problem in the western United States. An AML fund has been generated to pay for the cleanup and reclamation of land of older mines that were abandoned prior to the existence of regulations. The federal government gives half of the funds collected to the state the mine is located in to help with the reclamation effort. The other half is used by the Office of Surface Mining to respond to emergencies such as landslides, land subsidence, and fires, and to carry out high-priority cleanups in states without approved programs.

Abandoned Mines—A Worldwide Issue

Mining is an economic activity that has been practiced in the Americas for hundreds (in some cases, thousands) of years due to the region's rich deposits, which include gold, silver, and copper. However, the need for mine closures has become an issue. As more is understood concerning health, safety, and environmental issues, mines are being reevaluated for closure and clean up in order to protect the environment on a long-term basis.

The United Nations Environment Programme (UNEP), in 2001, supported the notion that abandoned mine sites have become an international problem, made even more difficult because of the associated financial and legal liability implications—in other words, determining who is responsible to pay for, and clean up, the mess. Their workshop in 2001 was a historical event because it was the first international meeting to consider the many issues surrounding the topic of abandoned mines. It was attended by government representatives of 10 countries. Their goal was to look at critical issues facing all countries: What are the environmental and social risks related to abandoned mines? What kind of criteria are needed to prioritize these risks? Is a regional or global inventory a prerequisite for action? What are the legal liability issues? What types of financial mechanisms exist? Most important, who will pay to clean up these sites?

The environmental, social, and economic problems associated with abandoned mine sites are serious and global. They affect all mining countries, including Brazil, Canada, France, Philippines, South Africa, the United States, and many others. The identified physical impacts of abandoned mine sites include altered landscapes; open pits and shafts; land no longer usable due to loss of soil, pH, or slope of the land; abandoned tailings dumps; changes in groundwater function; contaminated soils, water, and aquatic sediments; subsidence; and changes in vegetation. These problems have serious social and economic impacts on countries and individual communities due to loss of productive land, loss or degradation of groundwater, pollution of surface water by sediments or salts, poisoning of fish by contaminated sediments, degradation of river health, air pollution from dust or toxic gases, risk of people or animals falling into open shafts and pits, and landslides.

Some countries are starting to address these issues and explore innovative approaches to dealing with abandoned mine sites by considering how to do the following: (1) share responsibility, (2) make adjustments to land use, (3) maximize the potential for other commercial purposes, (4) develop economic and efficient cleanup

Abandoned mines are a serious threat to public safety and the environment. Government agencies are working on cleaning the mines, which are often located in areas that are easily accessible to the public. This photo shows acid mine water discharge from an abandoned mine in Montana. *(Photo by Stuart Jennings, Montana State. American Geological Institute, http://www.earthscienceworld.org/images)*

techniques, and (5) set goals to begin actively and systematically cleaning up sites.

In the United States alone, the Bureau of Land Management (BLM) has estimated that there are between 100,000 and 500,000 or more small

Contaminated mine waste creates long-lasting scars on the landscape. This photo shows acid mine discharge from underground workings prior to remediation in the Heddleston Mining District, Montana. *(Photo by Stuart Jennings, Montana State. American Geological Institute, http://www.earthscienceworld .org/images)*

and mid-sized abandoned hard rock mines in the western states alone. Most sites are not currently posing problems, but of those that are, 25% relate to health and safety matters, and 5% to environmental matters, primarily issues of water pollution. There are some 13,000 abandoned coal mines, mostly small and mid-sized, in the eastern states. These are causing mainly health and safety problems.

The principle environmental issues relate to water pollution, soil **erosion**, and soil contamination. There are also social and health-related impacts and safety issues. There are cultural, heritage, and visual impacts. One of the biggest threats is the increase in recreational traffic in areas with abandoned mines. As people venture further into wilderness or recreational areas—such as riding the increasingly popular all-terrain off-road vehicles—they are more likely to find themselves in dangerous situations with open shafts in the ground to fall into and toxic chemicals causing pollution in these areas.

Reclamation costs are excessive, and the United States is looking at government programs related to public awareness and outreach; cleanup (especially of safety hazards); water quality and hazardous materials monitoring; and science and research initiatives with government and educational institutions, such as universities.

Abandoned mine reclamation will take the combined efforts of many different types of professionals because the impacts of these sites are diverse. They involve ownership issues; legal issues; climatic conditions; wildlife that has taken up residence in abandoned sites; and archaeological, cultural, and historic preservation issues. It will take the continued and combined efforts of many different disciplines to solve this huge problem.

CHEMICAL CONTAMINATION—ACID MINE DRAINAGE

Acid mine drainage (AMD) is the drainage of highly acidic water that contains high levels of dissolved metals flowing from mine sites. The sites can be coal mines, surface mines, underground mines, or waste piles. The acidity is the result of sulfide minerals being exposed to the air (called oxidation). Acid mine drainage poses a serious environmental hazard because it can contaminate the soil, water, and air, which in turn impacts people, animals, and plants.

There are many types of sulfide minerals, but the iron sulfides, such as pyrite and maracasite (FeS_2), are common in coal regions and are the main AMD producers. When contaminants are exposed to water and oxygen, pyretic minerals oxidize to form acidic, iron- and sulfate-rich drainage.

The quality of the water that drains from underground mines or backfills of surface mines depends on the acid-producing (sulfide) and alkaline (carbonate) minerals that are contained in the disturbed rock. The areas that are richer in sulfide materials are the areas that are the most toxic, because these materials produce acid.

The acidity in abandoned mine areas occurs as two types: (1) mineral acidity, and (2) hydrogen **ion** acidity. Mineral acidity depends on the specific geologic materials in the area. For example, the presence of iron, aluminum, and manganese are important in the occurrence of acidity.

According to scientists at Lehigh University in Pennsylvania, approximately 12,428 miles (20,000 km) of streams and rivers in the United States are degraded by AMD. This is critical, because if AMD is not treated, the surface and groundwater sources will continue to be contaminated, causing serious health effects for people and polluting the ecosystems they live in. The detrimental results include contaminated drinking water; negative impacts on plants and animals that live by and in the rivers; and corrosion and weakening of bridges, monuments, and buildings nearby.

One example of this problem is found in the Wasatch Mountains in Utah (part of the Rocky Mountain chain). Before mining was strictly regulated, many prospectors worked the canyons in the area in search of gold, silver, and copper. Thousands of these mines have been abandoned, many of them over 100 years old. Many are on federal lands. In one instance, the U.S. Forest Service closed off a mine so that hikers could not go inside and fall down the shafts, but the area was never cleaned up. Today, the drainage leaking from the mine's opening is contaminated with acid mine drainage. This toxic drainage impacts the soil, surface water, and groundwater in the area. Not only is the watershed located in a drainage designated for municipal drinking water, but the area is also adjacent to a designated wilderness area and has a rich ecosystem of plants and a wide diversity of wildlife, such as cougar, bobcat, moose, deer, elk, raccoon, beaver, squirrels, and chipmunks. Currently, federal government agencies, such as the U.S. Forest Service and the BLM are cleaning up these mines, but the process is very expensive and involved and will take a long time to remediate (clean up) the tens of thousands of abandoned mines that exist on federal lands.

Fortunately, there are existing methods to treat this toxic drainage. Different chemicals can be added to water. The specific types of conditions—such as acidity levels, water flow, types of metals, degree of treatment needed, and desired final water quality—ultimately determine which chemicals will work best for a given mine. This makes each cleanup effort unique. The key to fixing the problem is to add enough alkalinity to raise water pH and supply hydroxides (OH-). This enables the dissolved metals in the water to form insoluble metal hydroxides and settle out of the water. The pH required to precipitate most metals from water ranges from pH 6 to 9 (in the pH scale, the two ends of the scale represent total acidity on one end and total alkalinity on the other, making the goal to shift the acidic conditions to the alkaline side). In these applications, treatment must be carefully monitored until desired results are reached.

There is also a passive approach to treat AMD through the use of aerobic wetlands. An aerobic wetland is a large surface area pond with horizontal surface flow. The pond is planted with wetland vegetation, such as cattails. Aerobic wetlands, however, can only treat water that is entirely alkaline. In this system, metals are precipitated through oxidation reactions to form oxides and hydroxides. Aerating the water before it reaches the wetland, by having it travel down falls and rapids in order to add oxygen to it, increases the efficiency of the process. In this method, iron content is reduced and the pH is lowered because of the addition of oxygen to the water.

REHABILITATION OF THE LAND

Mining disturbs the land. Because of this, it is important that current mines reclaim the surface during and after mining is completed and return the land to useful purposes. Oftentimes, when the rehabilitation is carefully planned and carried out, the reclaimed mine lands are more attractive to wildlife and for human uses than before mining started.

There are many ways of managing and fixing erosion caused by mining activities. Sediment carried by rainfall is one of the most serious environmental hazards of surface mining. Under current laws set by the Environmental Protection Agency, all surface water flowing off disturbed areas of the mine must be routed through sediment ponds. These ponds slow the flow of water and reduce erosion. Another way to control erosion is through the use of rocks (riprap). In this technique, drainage channels are lined with rock so that rapidly flowing water will be quickly slowed. The rocks also protect the soil underneath from eroding. The use of jute matting is another popular erosion control technique. Jute matting is a loosely woven "blanket" made from jute fibers; it resembles a very loose potato, or burlap, sack. In this method, drainages are lined with a jute mat to protect the soil under it from erosion and contamination. Depending on the topography and geologic materials in the area, different erosion-control techniques are used in different situations.

Fortunately, there are many practices in use today to reclaim mined lands. Each area is unique and the most effective reclamation practices are tailored to suit the specific area. Some surface mines may be cleaned up; the area graded; and trees, shrubs, and grasses planted. Other areas of mined land have been converted back to range for livestock grazing. Some reclaimed land has been successfully converted into areas suitable for wildlife habitat. Other mined areas have been converted into fish hatcheries or conditioned to become suitable for farming and used to

Reclamation of a mining site. The areas in the photo are revegetation test plots of the Streambank Tailing and Revegetation Study (STARS) at Ramsay Flats in Montana. *(Photo by Stuart Jennings, Montana State. American Geological Institute, http://www.earthscienceworld.org/images)*

grow hay and provide pasture for livestock. Others have become prairies. Whatever the physical characteristics of the land—flat, hilly, rocky, vegetated—serious and well-planned reclamation and rehabilitation efforts can contain and improve previously mined lands.

In order to successfully rehabilitate the land, several things must happen. All mine openings and underground workings must be permanently sealed off so that there are no open pits or similar features that could harm humans, animals, or the environment. All the material plus equipment left at the surface must be removed. Surface buildings and structures must be dismantled and removed from the site. Tailings, slurry ponds, waste dumps, stock piles, and any other surface features that might pose an environmental or human hazard must be cleaned up. The goal in rehabitation is to restore the surface land by leveling and revegetating it and returning natural water courses to their premined conditions.

The biggest issues facing rehabilitation today are the lack of clear legal and financial mechanisms and the lack of the willingness on the part of industry, governments, and communities to work together and form workable and productive partnerships. In order to be responsible stewards of the land, however, these problems must be overcome so that future generations will benefit.

CHAPTER 8

CONSERVATION OF MINERAL RESOURCES

This chapter examines the conservation of these precious resources. It begins by looking at new technology and its development and implementation; conflicts of interest in dealing with multiple land-use issues; possible effective substitutes to the use of existing mineral resources; the wisdom and benefits of reducing, reusing, and recycling mineral resources; and the issues involved in recycling metals.

NEW TECHNOLOGY AND ITS DEVELOPMENT

In a world with increasing population growth and a diminishing supply of natural resources, new technology is one of the most important developments that can ultimately lead to the conservation of mineral resources. In the past, when various mining technologies were just beginning, there was a lot of resource waste because the techniques of the time were not as refined and precise as they have become today. As technology becomes more refined and efficiency increases, mineral resources can be better conserved because needless waste can become better controlled.

Many major mining corporations worldwide have spent billions of dollars modernizing their current mining procedures and equipment in order to better conserve mineral resources. Besides lessening impacts to the environment, modernizing also helps reduce the price of acquiring the mineral commodity, which, in turn, helps the economy. If it costs less to produce, it costs less to buy. Modernizing also increases the safety levels at mining operations in addition to making mining processes more efficient. It also better controls the wastes and emissions coming from mining operations.

Current conservation practices strive to maximize efficiency, minimize production loss, and maximize the efficient use of water, energy, and raw materials. It also includes striving to minimize the release of pollutants to the environment and minimize waste through the use of current technology, technical innovation, best management practices, and employee involvement. By conserving and increasing efficiency, many mining companies believe the life span of mines and the precious mineral resources they contain can be significantly expanded.

Many specialists believe the key to mining in the future is the development of new technology. Advances in technology—such as 3-D seismic analysis, deep-water and high-angle drilling, hydraulic fracturing, and multilateral wells connected to a single bore—will allow mineral deposits to be imaged with better precision, extracted at reasonable costs, and obtained more efficiently.

New technology will not only increase the efficiency of mining, but also it will disturb less ground because less-invasive techniques will have to be used. By improving the efficiency by which minerals are found and obtained, the supply of these nonrenewable resources will be extended for use now and well into the future.

As geologists and other specialists discover more about the many complicated processes that occur beneath the Earth's surface, other mineral resources will be discovered. In addition, new technology will eventually allow mining engineers to mine deeper in the Earth.

Currently, many known mineral concentrations in the Earth are not accessible with current mining techniques, many of which cannot reach any deeper than 0.6 miles (1 km) below the Earth's surface. New technology will allow less-invasive processes to be developed that could even mine minerals in sensitive areas, such as major population centers, areas of natural beauty, or areas with fragile environments. Many specialists believe that in the future technological advances need to increase mining depth and safe accessibility, while at the same time remain economically feasible with as little environmental impact as possible.

CONFLICTS OF INTEREST— MULTIPLE LAND-USE ISSUES

Another major conservation issue concerns public lands and the multiple ways they are used. Federally owned land, administered by the U.S. government, is considered public land. These lands are managed for many uses that can occur simultaneously in order to provide the best use of these areas for the most people. For example, an area with mountains, rivers, or lakes might provide recreational benefits for people, as well as environmental benefits for wildlife and ecosystems, if managed properly. Other areas may consist of open prairie and provide grazing opportunities for cattle and sheep owned by ranchers who have leased land from the federal government for this purpose. These very same areas may also be rich in mineral resources, and those interested in obtaining these resources may want to lease the land from the federal government to set up mining operations.

Most land is suitable for multiple uses, such as recreational activities (hiking, camping, boating, fishing, rafting, canoeing), sources of clean water, wildlife (both terrestrial and aquatic), and minerals. The federal government does its best to try to meet the needs of all U.S. citizens, while at the same time providing responsible management and stewardship of the land.

A problem has emerged recently, however, that has made many people concerned about the future of the environment and the role

Oil and gas exploration is one of the many uses of public lands. *(Courtesy of Bureau of Land Management)*

the government is playing in it—the current worldwide energy situation. Due to rising energy costs, political unrest in the Middle East (the source of most of the world's petroleum), and increased environmental awareness, the government is looking for new energy sources within the United States—both conventional and renewable energy resources. Because of this, many places—particularly in the West—are being looked at for potential oil and gas drilling, as well as oil shale, coal, and tar sands recovery. Many Americans are concerned about impacts to the environment if large operations are begun for new mineral exploration and development.

Of particular concern are areas that have intangible value, such as wilderness potential and natural scenic beauty. Oftentimes, some of the most beautiful natural landscapes have vast resources of coal, oil, gas, and other minerals buried under them. Whether to develop these mineral resources is a source of controversy. One example of this is the Grand Staircase-Escalante National Monument in southern Utah, signed into existence by President Bill Clinton in 1996. Although many citizens were happy to see the monument designated (which protects the land from mineral development), others felt the opposite. Geologists at the Bureau of Land Management (the agency who manages the monument) have determined that the value of known and potential energy and mineral

How Many Minerals and Elements Are Necessary to Make a Computer?

It takes more than 33 elements and minerals to make a computer. Those vital computer ingredients consist of the following:

Aluminum	Lanthanides	Silver
Antimony	Lithium	Strontium
Barite	Manganese	Tantalum
Beryllium	Mercury	Tellurium
Cobalt	Mica	Tin
Columbium	Molybdenum	Tungsten
Copper	Nickel	Vanadium
Gallium	Platinum	Yttrium
Germanium	Quartz crystals	Zinc
Gold	Rhenium	Zirconium
Indium	Selenium	
Iron	Silicon	

The petroleum industry is involved in making computers because all the components noted above are made from plastic, which is a petroleum product.

(Source: Minerals Information Institute)

resources in the monument is between $223 billion and $330 billion at today's prices. This figure does not include the value of tar sands, carbon dioxide reserves, or any of the other mineral deposits, such as titanium, zirconium, uranium, or copper. The following is a listing of the value of specific resources within the monument area alone:

- Coal $221 billion–$312 billion
- Coal-bed gas $2 billion–$17.5 billion
- Petroleum $20 million–$1.1 billion
- Minerals $4.5 million and more.

The monument extends across 1.7 million acres of some of the most energy-rich lands in the lower 48 states. Heated debates occur over the pros and cons of protecting (conserving) the lands' mineral resources versus utilizing them to their fullest economic potential—an issue that will not likely be resolved soon. These are the issues that future land managers will have to consider when trying to find the right balance concerning conservation and land use.

SUBSTITUTES FOR MINERAL RESOURCES

Another way of conserving nonrenewable resources is to find substitutes. Although some of these substitutes may be other minerals, there are options available to conserve certain minerals over others. According to the Minerals Information Institute, the following minerals have these associated substitutes:

- Aluminum and bauxite—Even though aluminum is very important in industry and everyday applications, other commodities can replace it. For instance, copper can replace aluminum in electrical applications. Paper, plastics, and glass make packaging alternatives. Magnesium, titanium, and steel can be used in vehicles and other forms of ground and air transportation. Unless energy costs should rise steeply, however, the use of aluminum in most of these applications is not likely to become a serious issue. Worldwide sources of bauxite are still large enough to supply the demand for aluminum.

- Antimony–For the production of paint, reasonable replacements include zinc, titanium, tin, and chromium. Instead of using antimony as a lead hardening agent, calcium, copper, cadmium, and sulfur could be used. As a fire retardant, organic compounds exist that are effective.
- Asbestos–Because it has serous health implications, other materials must be used instead of asbestos. Ceramic fiber, glass fiber, steel fiber, and cellulose fiber are possible replacements.
- Bismuth–It can be replaced in applications for fire sprinkler systems and medical applications. For fire sprinklers, a glass bulb filled with glycerine is a workable alternative. In medical applications, certain antibiotics, magnesia, and alumina are suitable replacements.
- Copper–Alternatives today for copper pipes include a variety of plastic products. While copper wires have been key to the telecommunications industry over the years, it is now possible to use fiber optic cables instead. Aluminum can also substitute as a material to make wires.
- Lead–Suitable alternatives to lead include iron, tin, plastic, and aluminum.
- Lithium–For the production of ceramics and glass, potassium compounds have proven reliable. For use in batteries, successful substitutes include nickel, zinc, cadmium, and magnesium.
- Molybdenum–For use as a strengthening alloy in steel, boron, chromium, columbium, and vanadium are good substitutes.
- Silver–For silverware, stainless steel is a viable option; for the production of mirrors, rhodium and aluminum are acceptable substitutes.

DOING YOUR PART TO REDUCE WASTE

Every American throws away about 1,000 pounds (454 kg) of trash a year. The most effective way for consumers to help reduce the amount of energy and materials (which originate from mineral resources) consumed by industry is to decrease the number of unnecessary products purchased and to reuse items wherever possible. Purchasing only those items that are necessary, and reusing and recycling products, can reduce mineral use in the industrial sector.

Everyone can take an active role in reducing, reusing, and recycling materials. In order to reduce consumption, each person should buy only what he or she needs. Purchasing fewer goods means less to throw away. It also results in fewer goods being produced and less minerals being used in the manufacturing process. Buying goods with less packaging also reduces the amount of waste generated and the amount of energy and materials used.

Products should be bought that can be used over and over. If items are bought that can be reused, rather than disposable items that are used once and thrown away, it will save natural resources. It will also save the minerals used to make them and reduce the amount of landfill space needed to contain the waste.

Recycling should be a priority. Using recycled material almost always consumes less energy and materials than using new materials derived from minerals. Recycling reduces energy needs for mining, refining, and many other manufacturing processes. According to the U.S. Department of Energy, recycling a pound of steel saves enough energy to light a 60-watt light bulb for 26 hours. Recycling a ton of glass saves the equivalent of 9 gallons (34 L) of fuel oil. Recycling aluminum cans saves 95% of the energy required to produce aluminum from bauxite. Recycling paper cuts energy usage in half.

Efficiency and conservation are key components of mineral sustainability—the concept that every generation should meet its mineral needs without compromising the mineral needs of future generations. Mineral sustainability focuses on long-term mineral strategies and policies that ensure adequate minerals to meet today's needs, as well as tomorrow's.

Sustainability also includes investing in research and development of advanced technologies for producing conventional energy sources, promoting the use of alternative energy sources, finding renewable substitutes for minerals currently being used, and encouraging sound environmental policies.

Every person can take an active role to help reduce waste at home by learning basic waste-saving habits. Products can be bought that come in concentrated forms or that use minimal packaging. Most products can be reused, repaired, recycled, or composted instead of being simply thrown away. For example, everyone can:

Reduce

- Buy the largest size package and products that do more than one thing—for example, shampoos that include conditioners; or detergents that already contain bleach.
- Buy concentrated products or compact packages, such as frozen juices, floor cleaners, and fabric softeners that can be mixed with water at home.
- Look for products with minimal packaging. This uses fewer natural resources, and there is less to throw away.
- When mowing the lawn, leave grass clippings on the ground instead of bagging them. This is also beneficial to the environment because grass clippings decompose quickly, and add nutrients to the soil.

Reuse

- Buy reusable products such as rechargeable batteries.
- Pass on magazines, catalogs, and books to neighbors, hospitals, schools, and nursing homes.
- Reuse plastic or glass containers for storing food, nails, and other items.

- Reuse plastic shopping bags, boxes, and lumber. These items can be used repeatedly.

Repair

- Try to repair before considering replacing lawn mowers, tools, vacuum cleaners, TVs, and other mechanical or electrical items.
- Donate items that cannot be repaired at home to local charities or vocational schools (someone there may be able to repair and use them).
- Keep appliances in good working order. Properly maintained appliances are less likely to wear out or break and will not have to be replaced as frequently.

Recycle

- Shop for items that are recyclable or made from recycled materials.
- Recycle newspapers, plastics, glass, and cans.
- If a recycling program does not exist in your community, contact community officials to see if one could be started.

Compost

- Compost yard and kitchen waste. Compost makes an excellent fertilizer and improves the soil.
- If there is no room for a compost pile, offer compostable materials to community composting programs or garden projects nearby.

(Information courtesy of the U.S. Department of Energy)

RECYCLING METALS

In the United States alone, more than 6 million tons (5,500,000 metric tons) of aluminum is used each year, and 50% of that is made from recycled aluminum products. While individual consumers play a large role in the recycling of aluminum—such as soda cans—the leading driver behind recycling is industry.

Many industrialized countries, such as the United States, have no mineral resources of bauxite (the principle ore that aluminum is made from). However, the United States is heavily involved in the process stages of aluminum production through the making of "downstream products." The table below lists the important metals used and recycled in the United States today.

Important Metals Used and Recycled in the United States

Type of metal	% Recycled
Aluminum	50
Antimony	43
Chromium	26
Cobalt	25
Copper	24
Gold	60
Iron and steel scrap	100
Lead	65
Magnesium metal	24
Mercury	16
Nickel	30
Platinum group metals	67
Selenium	20
Silver	49
Tin	35
Tungsten	33
Zinc	29

(Source: Minerals Information Institute)

Aluminum can recycling is now so efficient that it is possible for a soda to be purchased at a grocery store, brought home and consumed, recycled into a new aluminum can, filled with a product, stocked on a grocery store shelf, and sold again—all within 90 days.

Aluminum is the only packaging material that more than covers the cost of its own collection and processing at recycling centers. Aluminum recycling is popular because it involves a product that is common to many people. Today, 1 pound (0.45 kg) of aluminum can make approximately 34 cans.

According to the U.S. Department of Energy, in 2003, the United States recycled 73.8 million tons (67 million metric tons) of metal. Metals are important, reusable resources. Although the ultimate supply of metal is fixed by nature (because metal is a nonrenewable resource), human ingenuity helps determine the quantity available for use by improving the processes used in mining the primary (Earth) metal and processing the secondary (recycled) metal. Recycling provides many environmental benefits, such as energy savings, reduced volumes of waste, and reduced emissions.

Metals can be recycled from many different types of objects, such as used beverage cans, junked automobiles, appliances, used jet engine blades and vanes, junked machinery and ships, and metal from commercial buildings and industrial plants. Through careful conservation efforts, minerals can be available for future generations, but it is up to us to act now.

CONCLUSION: THE FUTURE OF MINERALS

Each day, new uses for minerals are discovered and developed. Increasing use, however, means increased pressure on these natural resources. The reality is that if humans deplete a nonrenewable resource now, the resource will not be available for future use. It is important that humans continue to find new ways to use minerals more efficiently and how to recycle, reuse, and conserve. This chapter examines the questions scientists are facing now: How many known mineral reserves do we have and how long (at present consumption rates) will they last? How many undiscovered minerals still exist? How will technology affect future mining and search methodologies? What about exploring the Moon and other planets or the deep sea for untapped mineral resources? And finally, what are green minerals and how do they fit into the future?

ESTIMATING MINERAL RESERVES

Several assumptions are made in order to estimate the reserves of a given mineral resource. When estimates are made, specialists often look at the historical use of the mineral resource and critically reexamine that area's potential for additional resources not yet discovered. Specialists also consider the role and impact that more effective extraction technologies, recycling, and substitutions will have on extending future resource use.

In the United States, the U.S. Geological Survey (USGS) uses a classification scheme that assesses the following: (1) the degree of certainty about the existence and magnitude of supplies of those materials, and (2) the economic feasibility of recovering them. *Reserves* are defined as those supplies known to exist and to be both economically and technologically recoverable at the present time. *Resources* are defined to include all known, inferred, and theoretically possible supplies of the same substances, whether or not they are now economically and technologically recoverable. Therefore, the resources of a given mineral include its reserves, plus additional quantities that may (or may not) at some time become reclassifiable as reserves.

UNDISCOVERED MINERAL RESOURCES

In addition to needing to know where to find other mineral resources—based on geologic and mineral-forming processes—there are other issues involved in locating and actually using these resources. Two key issues that may impact future mineral development are competing land uses and environmental degradation due to mining. Once likely mineral-forming areas are identified, engineering cost modeling is often used to estimate the feasibility of mining. Undiscovered mineral resources include both new deposits and known occurrences for which no reliable information about location, quantity, and quality is available. The USGS then conducts a geologic assessment to estimate the potential economic effects from development of these deposits. Estimates are based on the quantity and economic importance of minerals.

The USGS uses a Potential Supply Analysis to analyze any metallic mineral deposits that could possibly occur in a region. This analysis uses quantitative (mathematical) models to describe the tonnages and grades for these deposit types and also estimates the number of deposits that are still undiscovered. This type of modeling produces a "prediction" model. The model also takes into account social factors (impact on towns and people), physical factors (feasibility of getting access to the mineral, and how rich the ore is), current mining prices, future mineral prices, and future costs of new mining technologies. If a model determines a mine would not be cost effective for one reason or another, the mine is not considered for development. If conditions, technology, or demand changes in the future, mining at that site may become a possibility at that time.

Although scientists believe significant undiscovered mineral resources exist throughout the world, exploration is expected to concentrate first on top priority exploration targets—areas believed to have the most potential. Economically, this is the smartest approach. Once these areas are looked at, other more problematic areas would then be considered. Many specialists believe that, as technology improves, cheaper, more efficient mining practices will be developed and successfully used where current technology is still too costly.

Environmental considerations are also a critical part of the assessment. As new regulations are passed, areas could be restricted or eliminated from consideration due to being too close to towns, rivers, drinking-water sources, recreational areas, or other factors. Costs to reclaim mined lands may also be a factor that determines whether or not mining is feasible. Also, as new reclamation methods are developed, it may be possible to clean up sites that would not be economical to mine and reclaim today. Fortunately, mining operations today do not simply focus on obtaining the mineral, but focus on reclaiming the land, reducing impacts, and promoting environmental health. Responsible mining practices have come a long way in just a few decades.

All nations face issues involving supply and utilization of raw materials. In today's global economy, a country's economic security depends on maintaining adequate mineral resource supplies. Global use of mineral resources will continue to increase in the future because of the continuing increase in global population and the desire for, and efforts to, improve living standards worldwide. In response to

Worldwide Nonfuel Resources

Country	Nonfuel resources
Africa	Aluminum, bauxite, diamonds, phosphate, copper, gold, iron, lead, uranium, nickel, platinum group, titanium, tungsten, zinc
Argentina	Gold, iron, gypsum, silver, zinc, uranium
Australia	Bauxite, aluminum, iron ore, copper, tin, silver, uranium, nickel, tungsten, mineral sands, lead, zinc, diamonds, magnesite
Bangladesh	Titanium
Bhutan	Gypsum, calcium carbide
Bolivia	Gold, tin, manganese, cement, zinc
Brazil	Iron, copper, manganese, chromite, copper, alumina, beryllium, tin
Burma	Tin, antimony, zinc, copper, tungsten, lead, marble, limestone, gemstones
Cambodia	Gemstones, iron ore, manganese, phosphate
Canada	Salt, coal, gold, barite, copper, sulfur, silicon, zinc, tellurium, titanium, cobalt
Chile	Nitrogen, iron, copper, manganese, silver
Colombia	Nickel, silver, coal, iron, gold, cement
Congo Kinshasa	Gold, columbium, copper, tantalum, tin
East Timor	Gold, manganese, marble
Ecuador	Silver, gold, copper, zinc, cadmium
Europe (Eastern)	Sand, gravel, limestone, copper, iron, sulfur, uranium, lead
Europe (Western)	Graphite, gypsum, iron, magnesium, copper, dolomite, lead, iron, marble, zinc, cadmium, nickel, tungsten
Fiji	Gold, copper
Greenland	Platinum group metals, iron ore, rare earths, gold, graphite, chromite
India	Iron ore, manganese, mica, bauxite, titanium ore, chromite, diamonds, limestone-dolomite-marble, barite, cement, garnet, graphite, rare earth elements, salt, talc, wollastonite
Indonesia	Tin, nickel, bauxite aluminum, copper, gold, silver
Iran	Aluminum, lead, zinc, copper, chromite, iron, sulfur, cement
Laos	Gypsum, tin, gold, gemstones, potash

Malaysia	Tin, copper, iron ore, bauxite, rare earth elements
Marshall Islands	Deep seabed minerals
Mexico	Gold, molybdenum, zinc, lead, selenium, salt, diatomite, sulfur, manganese, bismuth
Nauru	Phosphate
Nepal	Quartz, copper, cobalt, iron ore
New Caledonia	Nickel, chrome, iron, cobalt, manganese, silver, gold, copper
New Zealand	Iron ore, sand, gold, limestone
Papua New Guinea	Gold, copper, silver, nickel
Peru	Gold, copper, silver, zinc, lead, iron, bismuth, cement, zinc
Philippines	Nickel, cobalt, silver, gold, salt, copper
Pitcairn Islands	Offshore manganese, iron, copper, gold, silver, zinc
Russia	Iron, salt, aluminum, copper, cobalt, nickel, zinc, molybdenum
Saudi Arabia	Gold, silver, copper, lead, zinc, cement
Solomon Islands	Gold, bauxite aluminum, phosphates, lead, zinc, nickel
Sri Lanka	Gemstones
Thailand	Tin, tungsten, tantalum, lead, gypsum, lignite, fluorite, cement, dolomite, feldspar, salt, kaolin, ball clay
Uruguay	Gold, iron, lime
Venezuela	Alumina, gold, diamond
Vietnam	Phosphate, manganese, bauxite aluminum, chromate, kaolin, silica sand, rare earth elements

(Source: U.S. Geological Survey)

this growing demand for information on the global mineral-resource base, the USGS is organizing a cooperative international project to assess the world's undiscovered nonfuel mineral resources, called the Global Mineral Resource Assessment Project (GMRAP). The principal objective of GMRAP is to outline the regional locations and esti-mate the probable amounts of the world's remaining undiscovered nonfuel mineral resources to a depth of 0.62 miles (1 km) below the Earth's surface. This is the first international project of its kind. The table on pages 152–153 summarizes nonfuel resources that have been identified worldwide.

FUTURE MINING AND SEARCH METHODOLOGIES

In order to meet the future world demand for minerals, scientists have been looking both to traditional and nontraditional sources. Besides the traditional methods of surface and underground mining, future mineral resources are being looked at in the oceans, on the Moon, and in outer space.

Ocean Mining

Research is currently being conducted on the ocean bottoms near hydrothermal vents for mineral resources. In areas where hot water is venting onto the ocean floor from the Earth's interior, high concentra-tions of dissolved metals occur. Scientists believe some of these met-aliferous sediments are huge, such as ones found on the Mid-Atlantic Ridge. About the size of a football stadium, these mineral deposits are estimated to contain millions of metric tons of various metals, such as copper, zinc, silver, and gold. Areas off the west coast of Canada contain mounds on the seafloor that contain 722 feet (220 m) of stacked sul-fide lenses, also with deposits of copper and zinc. According to the U.S. Geological Survey, advances in marine geology and deep-ocean tech-nology have combined to make it realistic to go more than 1.2 miles (2 km) underwater for gold and other mineral treasures.

Many specialists believe that ocean bottom mining will be more environmentally friendly than land-based mining operations, because seafloor mining avoids many of the problems associated with terrestrial (land) mining. For example, there is no acid drainage, because the acids are neutralized by the alkaline seawater. The mineral deposits are on the seafloor, so there would be no excavation with the resulting waste rock piles, and no permanent structures would be left behind.

Biological Leaching

Removal of materials by dissolving them away from solids is called leaching. Biological leaching—also called heap leaching—can be used to recover metals from their ores. In this process, bacterial leaching is first used to oxidize sulphide minerals. Cyanide solution is then used to leach the metals from the mineral heap.

The theory and practice of leaching has existed for many years; this process has been already used long term to separate metals from their ores. In heap leaching, the solid is in a stationary pile and the solvent percolates through it. Once it becomes concentrated at the bottom, it is then removed.

Nuclear Blasting

Nuclear blasting is another possible future mining method. In this method, a nuclear explosion is triggered beneath the surface of the Earth, releasing huge amounts of heat and pressure. Rock in the vicinity is melted, and rock up to 150 feet (46 m) away is shattered and crushed. The top of the cavity collapses to form a chimney about 400 feet (122 m) high. In experiments, this has created 200,000 tons (181,436 metric tons) of fragmented rock. The possible use of nuclear explosives include large-scale excavation, increasing the yield of oil wells, extraction of oil from tar sands, extraction of oil from oil shale, and power production and breaking up of large low-grade ore deposits. Environmental concerns, however, may restrict development of this method.

Moon Mining

Scientists have determined there are many natural elements located on the Moon. The table on page 156 lists the common known elements by percent weight.

By weight, moon rocks are about 40% oxygen. Heating the top 3 feet (1 m) of an acre of moon dust to 2,372°F (1,300°C) retrieves 3,000 to 3,500 tons (2,721 to 3,175 metric tons) of oxygen.

Mining helium from the moon has also caught the attention of scientists. It is believed that the extraction of 1.10 tons (1 metric ton) of helium-3—the equivalent amount of energy needed to provide about 1/25 of the annual U.S. electricity consumption—will require the mining of about one acre of the lunar surface to a depth of 9 feet (3 m). Some scientists envision the use of a self-contained mobile mining unit, which moves around the Moon's surface. Others envision a spiral mining configuration. With spiral mining, the mobile mining machine would be attached to the central station by a telescoping support arm. The miner would extract the lunar material by operating the mining arm. Using solar thermal energy, the arm would have the ability to

Mineral Composition of the Moon

Element	Percent by weight
Aluminum	7.3
Calcium	8.5
Chromium	0.2
Iron	12.1
Magnesium	4.8
Manganese	0.2
Oxygen	40.8
Potassium	0.1
Silicon	19.6
Sodium	0.3
Titanium	4.5
Total	98.4

(Source: National Aeronautics and Space Administration)

move, excavate, and process the mined material at refining subsystems located in the central control station.

Asteroid Mining

Scientists are also looking toward outer space for sources of minerals. One option that has received considerable attention lately is asteroid mining. This technique would process the ore on-site (in space) and bring back only the processed materials, as well as produce fuel propellant for the return trip.

An asteroid the size of a football stadium filled with ore (about 328 feet or 100 m wide, tall, and long), can contain 2,000,000 tons (1,814,369 metric tons) of material. The surface gravity of an asteroid this size would be practically zero—less than one ten-thousandth that of the Moon. The escape velocity would be 0.2 miles per hour (0.3 km per hour). Because of this, material could theoretically be easily moved around. In addition, erected structures are not subject to the force of gravity.

Staying attached to, and moving around, the asteroid could be accomplished by harpoons or anchors, or by using one or more cables around the asteroid with flat plates or rocks to keep the cable from digging in, or a net. With rocky asteroids, gripping the surface like a rock climber is a suggested method.

Some studies have suggested that the asteroid's rotation could be stopped in order to attach solar-powered processing equipment to the asteroid and have it always facing the Sun to employ solar power. An early NASA study recommended despinning the asteroid by anchoring a cable, wrapping it around the asteroid, and having a rocket-powered space Jeep slow it down and stop its rotation.

Theoretically, mining and processing an asteroid in space is less cumbersome than processing ore on Earth. Heavy mining and transport machinery is not needed; neither is complex chemical processing to get valuable materials. Waste disposal is done by putting the waste into a bag.

Experts believe a typical asteroid would have a crumbly texture, consisting of silicate embedded with nickel-iron. Proposed feasible mining methods include strip mining (scraping away at the asteroid's surface) or tunneling into the asteroid by digging and following specific ore veins.

One interesting mining concept—which is completely different than mining on Earth—takes advantage of the zero-gravity environment. A canopy is put around the mine site and a dust kicker goes down to the asteroid and just kicks up the ore at low velocity. When there is enough ore in the canopy, it is sealed off and moved to the processing site. This concept would be simple, reliable, and present minimal risk of breakdown of mining machinery.

Asteroidal material is very rich ore, requiring only minimal processing. Only basic ore processing needs to occur at the asteroid to produce metals, volatiles, minerals, glasses, and ceramics. The required equipment is basic. At an input chute, the ore is ground up and sieved into different sizes as the first step of the processing system. Simple mechanical grinders crush the ore into coarse blocks, and then a series of rollers for fine crushing are arranged in a slowly rotating housing to provide centrifugal movement of the material.

The streams of material are put through magnetic fields to separate the nickel-iron metals from the silicate grains. The nonmagnetic material is channeled into a solar oven where the volatiles are cooked out. In zero gravity and windless space, the oven mirrors can be huge and made of aluminum foil. The gas stream is piped to tanks located in space. Rocket fuel for the delivery trip to Earth's orbit can also be produced by separating oxygen and hydrogen gases from the mix.

Some silicate material from the asteroid can also be shipped back to Earth's orbit to be used for the manufacture of glass, fiberglass, ceramics, "astercrete," dirt to grow things in, and radiation shielding for habitats and sensitive silicon electronics.

Undesired material can be put in a large waste bag container of "sandbags" or cast into bricks by a solar oven or just removed from the mining operation. After the asteroid is entirely consumed, the equipment can be moved to the next asteroid to mine. A few onsite general engineers would be needed at the asteroid to set up teleoperation equipment and handle repairs. The workers would live in artificial gravity produced by connecting habitats by cable. All the chemicals necessary for breathing and drinking are abundant on asteroids, but a reserve of air, water, and getaway fuel would be kept on hand in case of an emergency.

OCEAN MINERAL RESOURCES—A NEW FRONTIER

More than 70% of the Earth is covered by ocean. Because relatively little exploration has occurred at deep-ocean depths, the ocean is considered, by many scientists, to be the Earth's final frontier. A wide variety of mineral resources are found on the seafloor. These resources fall into four general categories:

- Granular sediments
- Placer minerals
- Hydrothermal deposits
- Hydrogenetic minerals

Granular sediments are transported to the sea by rivers and glaciers and are sorted according to size by wave action on the coastline. They include quartz-rich sand and gravel, carbonate-rich sand, shell, silt, and clay. Gold, diamonds, platinum, tin, and titanium are among the most common placer minerals, as well as concentrations of heavy minerals and ores such as titanium oxide. Hydrothermal minerals are associated with volcanic activity and include sulfide deposits rich in copper, zinc, lead, gold, and silver. Hydrogenetic deposits form by precipitation from seawater under various conditions and provide minerals such as phosphorite, salt, barite, and iron-manganese nodules, and crusts rich in cobalt, platinum, nickel, copper, and rare earth elements.

The Outer Continental Shelf (OCS) of the United States is a significant source of oil and gas for the nation's energy supply. At the end of 2002, the U.S. offshore supplied more than 25% of the country's natural gas production and more than 30% of total domestic oil production. These U.S. offshore areas are estimated to contain significant quantities of resources in yet-to-be-discovered fields. Estimates currently stand at 76 billion barrels of oil and 406.1 trillion cubic feet (11.5 trillion cubic meters) of gas. According to the U.S. Department of Energy, these volumes represent about 60% of the oil and 41% of the natural gas resources estimated to be contained in remaining undiscovered fields in the United States.

The principal mineral resources presently being extracted and likely to be extracted in the near future are salt; potassium; magnesium; sand and gravel; limestone and gypsum; manganese nodules; phosphorites; metal deposits associated with volcanism and seafloor vents; placer gold, tin, titanium, and diamonds; and water itself. There is so much salt available in the oceans, experts believe it could supply all human needs for hundreds, even thousands, of years. Although salt is extracted directly from the oceans in many countries by evaporating the water and leaving the residual salts, most of the nearly 200 million metric tons of salt produced annually is mined from large beds of salt. These beds, now deeply buried, were formed long ago when waters from ancient oceans evaporated in shallow seas, leaving thick beds of salt behind. The beds were then covered and protected from solution and destruction. Potassium salts occur in many thick evaporite deposits along with common salt and tens of millions of metric tons per year are mined from these beds.

Magnesium, dissolved in seawater at a concentration of about 1,000 parts per million, is the only metal that can be directly extracted from seawater. Presently, approximately 60% of the magnesium metal and many of the magnesium salts produced in the United States are extracted from seawater electrolytically. The remaining portion of the magnesium metal and salts is extracted from ancient ocean deposits where the salts precipitated during evaporation.

Sand and gravel are key mineral resources found in the ocean. The ocean basins are a major depositional site of sediments eroded from the land; and beaches represent the largest residual deposits of sand. Although beaches and near-shore sediments are locally extracted for use in construction, they are generally considered too valuable as recreational areas to permit removal for construction purposes. For instance, a quarry would not be welcome on the beaches at Waikiki, in Honolulu, Hawaii. Nevertheless, older beach sand deposits are abundant on the continents, especially the coastal plains, where they are extensively mined for construction materials, glass manufacture, and preparation of silicon metal. Gravel deposits are processed for building materials.

Limestone (rock composed of calcium carbonate) forms in the tropical to semitropical oceans of the world today as the result of precipitation by biological organisms ranging from mollusks to corals and plants. The continents and tropical islands contain large deposits of limestone that are extensively mined. Much of the limestone is used directly in cut or crushed form, but much is also calcined (cooked) to be converted into cement. Gypsum forms during evaporation of seawater and can occur with evaporite salts with limestone. Gypsum deposits are mined and converted into plaster of Paris and used for construction.

Manganese nodules have received a lot of attention lately as a valuable mineral resource. The deep ocean floors of the Atlantic and Pacific Oceans contain large quantities of these nodules. Despite their name, they usually contain more iron than manganese. They do, however, represent the largest known resource of manganese. These potato-sized, dark, round nodules also contain nickel, copper, cobalt, and other minerals. The nodules were first discovered on the famous oceanographic *Challenger* expedition of the 1870s. Steel production requires millions of tons of manganese annually. Though ocean mining for manganese nodules has generated a great deal of interest, several factors have served as obstacles, including the difficult ocean terrain, the high cost, and political and international disputes over rights to mine the mineral. Consequently, these rich deposits largely remain as potential resources for the future.

Phosphorites are another important mineral resource from the deep ocean. Complex organic and inorganic processes constantly precipitate phosphate-rich crusts and granules in shallow marine environments. They represent future potential reserves if land-based deposits become depleted.

Submarine investigations of oceanic rift zones have revealed that rich deposits of zinc and copper, with associated lead, silver, and gold, are forming at the sites of hot hydrothermal features commonly called black smokers. These metal-rich deposits, ranging from chimney- to pancake-like, form where deeply circulating seawater has dissolved metals from the underlying rocks and spreads out onto the cold seafloor along major fractures. The deposits forming today are not being mined because of their remote locations and the constraints of difficult access.

Placer deposits of gold, tin, titanium, and diamonds are also found in the ocean. Today, much of the world's tin and many of the gem diamonds are recovered by dredging near-shore ocean sediments for minerals that were carried into the sea by rivers. Gold has been recovered in the past from such deposits, most notably in Nome, Alaska. Large quantities of placer titanium minerals occur in beach and near-shore sediments, but mining today is confined generally to the beaches of onshore deposits because of the higher costs and environmental constraints of marine mining.

The world's oceans, with a total volume of more than 119,956,379 cubic miles (500 million cubic kilometers), hold more than 97% of all the water on Earth. However, the 3.5% salt content of this water makes it unusable for most human needs. The extraction of freshwater from ocean water has been carried out for many years, but provides only a very small portion of the water used and is expensive compared to land-based water resources. Technological advances, especially in reverse osmosis, continue to increase the efficiency of freshwater extraction.

Many scientists believe we are on the brink of the era of deep-ocean mining. Dr. Steven Scott, a geologist at the University of Toronto, in Toronto, Canada, says that advances in marine geology and deep-ocean technology have combined to make it realistic to go more than 1.2 miles (2 km) underwater for mineral resources.

Scott believes the key challenge for new marine-mining companies will be developing the technology to extract the ore from the watery

Deep-sea exploration is considered by many to be the last frontier for exploration on Earth. This is a photo of a high-tech submersible called CLELIA, which was constructed by Perry Oceanographics, preparing to launch for deep-sea exploration. *(Photo courtesy of NOAA/National Undersea Research Program)*

depths. He envisions the use of "deep-sea versions of robotic coal-mining machines" with the ore piped up to mining ships, or semisubmersible platforms, like those used by the offshore oil industry.

According to the National Oceanic and Atmospheric Administration, as deep-sea technology progresses, submersibles will be further refined and improved in order to explore the oceans for minerals. Currently, an underwater mining vehicle capable of mining and pumping sand from the ocean floor through a flexible riser system has been developed as the first step toward development of technology for deep-sea mining.

As scientific advances occur, minerals will continue to reveal future applications and uses. The key to discovering new applications lies in conserving present resources and giving science and technology an opportunity to reach their full potential. *(Courtesy of Nature's Images)*

GREEN MINERALS—THE WAY OF THE FUTURE

To maintain and improve current standards of living, society will need fresh supplies of metals and minerals for many generations to come. With continually increasing populations, recycling will help maintain a source of minerals and metals, but it is not the complete answer. Because of this, it is critical that specialists find the cleanest, most efficient, and environmentally safe ways to extract and process minerals and to recycle used metals. This issue goes beyond any single country—it is an important global issue. Many scientists believe the ultimate goal is to achieve an "industrial ecology," in which industry produces no waste at all, and all its byproducts from various processes are used productively in other industrial processes and then recycled.

According to CSIRO Mineral in Australia, the concept of *zero waste* is geared toward eliminating waste from the production and processing of minerals (i.e., whatever is taken from nature will be made into something useful). In some processes, this waste will be treated and fed back into the process; in others it will become the feedstock for a downstream industry. For example, iron ore tailings are a possible feedstock for making iron or steel. By applying this concept, many people are hopeful that the ultimate goal of zero waste and maximum sustainability will be reached. Scientists are working on processes to apply these concepts to several different commodities, such as producing green (environmentally friendly) steel and gold. They are also looking at new technologies that would allow water to be extracted from coal as a by-product that could then be used in other industrial processes, such as in power generating stations.

As illustrated throughout this book, minerals affect our lives every day and the standard of living we currently enjoy would not be possible without them. From cars to copper wiring in computers to glass bottles and highly-sophisticated electronic devices, to homes and modes of transportation, to the salt we add to our food and the dietary supplements we may take—minerals are all around us. If we are to continue to enjoy the luxuries and benefits minerals bring, then society as a whole must learn now how to conserve them to ensure their existence for the generations of the future.

Common Elements

Element	Symbol	Metal or nonmetal	State at room temperature
Hydrogen	H	Nonmetal	Gas
Helium	He	Nonmetal	Gas
Lithium	Li	Metal	Solid
Carbon	C	Nonmetal	Solid
Nitrogen	N	Nonmetal	Gas
Oxygen	O	Nonmetal	Gas
Fluorine	F	Nonmetal	Gas
Neon	Ne	Nonmetal	Gas
Sodium	Na	Metal	Solid
Magnesium	Mg	Metal	Solid
Aluminum	Al	Metal	Solid
Silicon	Si	Metalloid	Solid
Phosphorus	P	Nonmetal	Solid
Sulfur	S	Nonmetal	Solid
Chlorine	Cl	Nonmetal	Gas
Argon	Ar	Nonmetal	Gas
Potassium	K	Metal	Solid
Calcium	Ca	Nonmetal	Solid
Iron	Fe	Metal	Solid
Copper	Cu	Metal	Solid
Zinc	Zn	Metal	Solid
Bromine	Br	Nonmetal	Liquid
Silver	Ag	Metal	Solid
Tin	Sn	Metal	Solid
Iodine	I	Nonmetal	Solid
Gold	Au	Metal	Solid
Mercury	Hg	Metal	Liquid
Lead	Pb	Metal	Solid

The Reactivity Series

Metal	Air	Water	Acid
Potassium	Burns easily	Reacts with cold water	Violent reaction
Sodium	Burns easily	Reacts with cold water	Violent reaction
Calcium	Burns easily	Reacts with cold water	Violent reaction
Magnesium	Burns easily	Reacts with steam	Very reactive
Aluminum	Reacts slowly	Reacts with steam	Very reactive
Zinc	Reacts slowly	Reacts with steam	Quite reactive
Iron	Reacts slowly	Reacts with steam	Quite reactive
Lead	Reacts slowly	Reacts slowly with steam	Reacts very slowly
Copper	Reacts slowly	No reaction	No reaction
Silver	No reaction	No reaction	No reaction
Gold	No reaction	No reaction	No reaction

Mineral Habits
(The characteristic crystal form or combination of forms of a mineral)

Habit	Habit description
Acicular	Occurs as needlelike crystals
Aggregates	Made of numerous individual crystals or clusters
Amorphous	No crystalline form or imitative shape
Anhedral grains	Granular minerals without the expression of crystal shapes
Arborescent	Treelike growths of branched systems
Bitter taste	Bitter taste from water soluble magnesium or calcium compounds
Bladed	Aggregates of thin lath-like crystals
Blocky	Crystal shape tends to be equant
Blocky-rhombohedral	Crystal shape resembles a rhombohedron

Mineral Habits *(continued)*
(The characteristic crystal form or combination of forms of a mineral)

Habit	Habit description
Botryoidal	Grapelike rounded forms
Capillary	Very slender and long, like a thread or hair
Cleavable	Easily cleaved into fragments
Cog-wheel	Generally six-sided twinned crystals forming cog-wheel shapes
Colloform	Forming from a gel or colloidal mass
Columnar	Forms columns
Comb	Drusy layers deposited on top of each other to produce a toothed structure
Compact	Occurs as a compact mass
Concretionary	Rounded massive fine-grained materials
Cruciform	Twinned tabular crystals with a crosslike outline
Cryptocrystalline	Occurs as crystals too small to distinguish with the naked eye
Crystalline-coarse	Occurs as well-formed, coarse-sized crystals
Crystalline-fine	Occurs as well-formed, fine-sized crystals
Crystalline-poor	Occurs primarily as crudely formed crystals
Cubic crystals	Occurs as cubic-shaped crystals
Cylindrical	Shaped like a cylinder
Deliquescent	Crystals absorb water from the air and melt or otherwise deteriorate
Dendritic	Branching treelike growths of great complexity
Disseminated	Occurs in small, distinct particles dispersed in matrix
Divergent	Crystals radiate from a center without producing stellar forms

Druse	Crystal growth in a cavity which results in numerous crystal-tipped surfaces
Earthy	Dull, clay-like texture with no visible crystalline affinities
Efflorescences	Crystals covering matrix, generally produced from transpiroevaporation
Encrustations	Forms crustlike aggregates on matrix
Euhedral crystals	Occurs as well-formed crystals showing good external form
Fan Shaped	Occurs as radiating crystals shaped like a fan
Fibrous	Crystals made up of fibers
Flakes	Flat, thin crystals or aggregates
Foliated	Two-dimensional platy forms
Friable	Loosely cohesive material that granulates (crumbles) with your fingers
Globular	Spherical, or nearly so, rounded forms
Granular	Generally occurs as anhedral to subhedral crystals in matrix
Hexagonal	Six-sided crystal shape in cross-section or habit
Inclusions	Generally found as inclusions in other minerals
Indistinct	Crystals or grains are unremarkable or poorly formed; anhedral to subhedral crystals
Intergrown crystals	Occurs as intergrown crystalline aggregates
Irregular grains	Occurs as splotchy, anhedral crystals forming inclusions in other minerals or rocks
Lamellar	Thin laminae producing a lamellar structure
Lath	Shaped like a small, thin plaster lath, tabular (rectangular) in shape
Liquid	Occurs as a liquid at room temperatures
Mammillary	Larger "breast-like" founded forms resembling botryoidal

Mineral Habits *(continued)*
(The characteristic crystal form or combination of forms of a mineral)

Habit	Habit description
Massive	Uniformly indistinguishable crystals forming large masses
Massive-fibrous	Distinctly fibrous fine-grained forms
Massive-granular	Common texture observed in granite and other igneous rock
Massive-lamellar	Distinctly foliated fine-grained forms
Metamict	Mineral originally crystalline, now amorphous due to radiation damage
Micaceous	Platy texture with "flexible" plates
Microscopic crystals	Crystals visible only with microscopes
Mossy	Like moss in form or appearance
Nodular	Tuberose forms having irregular protuberances over the surface
Nuggets	Irregular lumps produced by stream transport of malleable metals
Octahedral crystals	Occurs as octahedral-shaped crystals
Oolitic	<0.12 inch (<3 mm) rounded spherical grains
Pistolitic	>0.12 inch (>3 mm) rounded spherical grains
Platy	Sheet forms
Plumose	Micalike minerals forming aggregates of plumelike forms
Porcelainous	Fine-grained, translucent massive material like broken china
Powdery	Forms a loose, poorly coherent pulverulent mass
Prismatic	Crystals shaped like slender prisms
Pseudocubic	Crystals show a cubic outline
Pseudomorphous	Occurs in the form of another mineral

Pseudooctohedral	Crystals show an octahedral outline
Pseudoorthorhombic	Crystals show an orthorhombic shape
Pseudorhombohedral	Crystals show a rhombohedral outline
Pseudotetragonal	Crystals show a tetragonal shape
Pseudohexagonal	Crystals show a hexagonal outline
Pulverulent	Forms a loose, poorly coherent powdery mass
Pyramidal	Crystals are shaped like pyramids
Radial	Crystals radiate from a center without producing stellar forms
Reniform	Kidneylike in shape
Reticulate	Fibers or columns cross in netlike crystalline growths
Rhombohedral crystals	Occurs as well-formed crystals showing rhobohedral crystals
Rosette	Bundled tabular aggregates resembling rose flower petals
Scaly	Morphology like fish scales
Skeletal	Crystals form crude outlines with missing faces
Spherical	Spherical, rounded aggregates
Square	Occurs as square crystals in shape or outline
Stalactitic	Shaped like pendant columns as stalactites or stalagmites
Stellate	Occurs as spherical, radial aggregates radiating from a starlike point
Striated	Parallel lines on crystal surface or cleavage face
Subhedral crystals	Occurs as crystals which tend to exhibit a recognizable crystal shape
Sugary	Granular texture formed from small, anhedral to subhedral grains forming massive rock
Tabular	Form dimensions are thin in one direction

Mineral Habits   *(continued)*
(The characteristic crystal form or combination of forms of a mineral)

Habit	Habit description
Tarnishes	Freshly fractured surfaces form a surface oxidation film
Thin	Flat-dimensioned crystals
Triangular crystals	Occurs as triangular-shaped crystals
Twinning common	Crystals are usually twinned
Very soluble	Material dissolves readily in water leaving no residue
Water soluble	Water soluble mineral
Waxy	Looks like candle wax
Wedge-shaped	Crystals shaped like a wedge
Wheat sheaf	Bundle-shaped aggregates resembling wheat sheafs after hand reaping

Mineral Luster
(The reflection of light from the surface of a mineral)

Luster	Luster description
Adamantine	High index of refraction
Adamantine-greasy	Between adamantine and greasy
Adamantine-metallic	Between adamantine and metallic
Adamantine-pearly	Between pearly and adamantine
Adamantine-resinous	Between resinous and adamantine
Adamantine-silky	Between silky and adamantine
Chatoyant	Numerous hairlike inclusions aligned to produce "cat's eye" figure
Earthy (dull)	Completely dull

Greasy (oily)	Surface alteration
Metallic	Specular reflection
Metallic-dull	Has a dull metallic luster
Pearly	Formed by numerous partly developed cleavages
Resinous	Luster of resin
Resinous-greasy	High index of refraction with surface alteration
Resinous-metallic	High index of refraction in nearly opaque minerals
Schiller	Caused by numerous platy inclusions or separations
Silky	Noticeable shiny direction
Silky-pearly	Silky and pearly lusters
Submetallic	Almost metallic reflection
Subadamantine	Not quite adamantine in luster
Vitreous (glassy)	Luster of broken glass
Vitreous-adamantine	Has aspects of both vitreous and adamantine lusters
Vitreous-dull	Has aspects of both vitreous and dull lusters
Vitreous-greasy	Has aspects of both vitreous and greasy lusters
Vitreous-metallic	Has aspects of both vitreous and metallic lusters
Vitreous-pearly	Has aspects of both vitreous and pearly lusters
Vitreous-resinous	Has aspects of both vitreous and resinous lusters
Vitreous-silky	Has aspects of both vitreous and silky lusters
Vitreous-waxy	Has aspects of both vitreous and waxy lusters
Waxy	Fairly dull luster

Mineral Fracture
(The way in which a mineral breaks)

Fracture	Fracture description
Brittle	Generally displayed by glasses and most nonmetallic minerals
Brittle-conchoidal	Very brittle fracture producing small, conchoidal fragments
Brittle-irregular	Very brittle fracture producing irregular fragments
Brittle-sectile	Brittle fracture with slightly sectile shavings possible
Brittle-splintery	Brittle fracture leaving splintery fragments
Brittle-subconchoidal	Brittle fracture with subconchoidal fragments
Brittle-uneven	Very brittle fracture producing uneven fragments
Conchoidal	Fractures developed in brittle materials characterized by smoothly curving surfaces
Conchoidal-irregular	Irregular fracture producing small, conchoidal fragments
Conchoidal-uneven	Uneven fracture producing small, conchoidal fragments
Earthy	Dull, claylike fractures with no visible crystalline affinities
Elastic	Fragments which spring back after bending
Even	Flat surfaces (not cleavage) fractured in an even pattern
Fibrous	Thin, elongated fractures produced by crystal forms or intersecting cleavages
Flexible	Flexible fragments
Fragile	Crystals with a delicate and easily injured structure
Friable	The crumbly disintegration of earthy materials or highly fractured minerals

Granular	Fracture surfaces produced by aggregated minerals
Hackly	Jagged, torn surfaces
Irregular	Flat surfaces (not cleavage) fractured in an irregular pattern
Malleable	Deforms rather than breaking apart with a hammer
Micaceous	Fracture of flexible micaceous cleavage fragments
None	No fractures
Plastic	Deforms like soft, plastic materials
Plastic-splintery	Thin, soft, flexible, elongated fractures produced by intersecting good cleavages or partings
Regular	Flat surfaces (not cleavage) fractured in a regular pattern
Sectile	Curved shavings or scrapings produced by a knife blade
Splintery	Thin, elongated fractures produced by intersecting good cleavages of partings
Subconchoidal	Fractures developed in brittle materials characterized by semicurving surfaces
Sugary	Fracture surfaces produced by finely aggregated minerals
Tough	Difficult to break apart as shown by fibrous minerals and most metals
Uneven	Flat surfaces (not cleavage) fractured in an uneven pattern
Unknown	Minerals too small to observe fractures
Weak	Hard to handle without causing serious harm or damage

STATE MINERAL PRODUCTION SUMMARIES

The minerals available in each state are listed below.

Alabama   Bauxite, Cement (portland), Clay, Coal, Iron Ore, Limestone, Marble, Mica, Salt, Sand and Gravel (construction), Stone (crushed), and Petroleum.

Alaska   Beryl, Coal, Gold, Iron Ore, Lead, Mercury, Molybdenum, Natural Gas, Petroleum, Platinum, Sand and Gravel (construction), Stone, Tungsten, Uranium, and Zinc.

Arizona   Asbestos, Cement (portland), Copper, Gold, Gypsum, Lead, Lime, Mercury, Molybdenum, Sand and Gravel (construction), Silver, Uranium, Vanadium, and Zinc.

Arkansas   Aggregate (crushed stone and gravel), Bauxite, Bromine Brine, Cement (portland), Coal, Diamonds, Gemstones, Gypsum, Natural Gas, Novaculite, Petroleum, Silica, and Tripol.

California   Asbestos, Borax, Bromine, Clay, Copper, Gold, Gypsum, Iron Ore, Lead, Lithium Magnesium, Marble, Mercury, Molybdenum, Natural Gas, Petroleum, Platinum, Potash, Rare Earths, Salt, Sand and Gravel (construction), Silver, Stone (crushed), Talc, Tungsten, and Zinc.

Colorado   Beryl, Cement (portland), Clay, Coal, Copper, Fluorspar, Gold, Iron Ore, Lead, Marble, Mica, Molybdenum, Natural Gas, Petroleum, Sand and Gravel (construction), Silver, Stone (crushed), Tungsten, Uranium, Vanadium, and Zinc.

Connecticut   Clay, Mica, Sand and Gravel (construction), Stone (crushed), Stone (dimensional), and Gemstones.

Delaware   Magnesium Compounds (from seawater), and Sand and Gravel (construction).

Florida   Cement (portland), Clay, Limestone, Peat, Phosphates, Sand and Gravel (construction), Stone (crushed), Titanium, and Zirconium.

Georgia   Barite, Bauxite, Cement (portland), Clay, Granite, Iron Ore, Manganese, Marble, Mica, Sand and Gravel (construction), Slate, Stone (crushed), Stone (dimension), Talc, and Titanium.

Hawaii   Cement (masonry), Cement (portland), Gemstones, Sand and Gravel (construction), and Stone (crushed).

Idaho   Antimony, Cobalt, Copper, Gold, Iron Ore, Lead, Mercury, Molybdenum, Phosphates, Sand and Gravel (construction), Silver, Thorium, Titanium, Vanadium, Tungsten, and Zinc.

Illinois   Cement (portland), Clay, Coal, Fluorspar, Lead, Limestone, Petroleum, Sand and Gravel (construction and industrial), Stone (crushed), and Zinc.

Indiana   Cement (masonry), Cement (portland), Clay, Coal, Gypsum, Limestone, Natural Gas, Petroleum, and Sand and Gravel (construction).

Iowa   Cement (portland), Clay, Coal, Gypsum, Limestone, Sand and Gravel (construction), and Stone (crushed).

Kansas   Cement (portland), Clay, Coal, Gypsum, Helium, Lead, Limestone, Natural Gas, Petroleum, Salt, Sand and Gravel (construction), Stone (crushed), and Zinc.

Kentucky   Cement (portland), Clay, Coal, Fluorspar, Limestone, Natural Gas, Petroleum, Sand and Gravel (construction), and Stone (crushed).

Louisiana   Gypsum, Natural Gas, Petroleum, Salt, Sand and Gravel (construction and industrial), Stone (crushed), and Sulfur.

Maine   Cement (masonry and portland), Clay, Mica, Peat, Sand and Gravel (construction), and Stone (crushed).

Maryland   Cement (masonry and portland), Clay, Coal, Limestone, Natural Gas, Peat, Sand and Gravel (construction), and Stone (crushed).

Massachusetts   Clays, Granite, Limestone, Sand and Gravel (construction), and Stone (crushed).

Michigan   Bromine, Cement (portland), Clay, Copper, Gypsum, Iron Ore, Limestone, Magnesium Compounds, Natural Gas, Peat, Petroleum, Potash, Salt, Sand and Gravel (construction), and Stone (crushed).

Minnesota   Clay, Cobalt, Copper, Granite, Iron Ore, Limestone, Manganese, Nickel, Sand and Gravel (construction and industrial), and Stone (crushed and dimensional).

Mississippi   Cement (portland), Clay, Iron Ore, Natural Gas and Petroleum, Sand and Gravel (construction and industrial), and Stone (crushed).

Missouri   Barite, Clay, Coal, Copper, Iron Ore, Lead, Limestone, Marble, Natural Gas, Silver, Stone (crushed), and Zinc.

Montana   Cement (portland), Copper, Gold, Graphite, Gypsum, Lead, Manganese, Natural Gas, Petroleum, Palladium, Phosphates, Platinum, Sand and Gravel (construction), Silver, Thorium, Tungsten, Vermiculite, and Zinc.

Nebraska   Cement (masonry and portland), Clay, Natural Gas, Petroleum, Sand and Gravel (construction and industrial), and Stone (crushed).

Nevada   Barite, Clay, Copper, Diatomite, Gold, Gypsum, Lead, Lithium, Magnesium, Mercury, Molybdenum, Petroleum, Salt, Sand and Gravel (construction), Silver, Sulfur, Tungsten, and Zinc.

New Hampshire   Beryl, Clays, Gemstones, Granite, Mica, Sand and Gravel (construction), Stone (crushed and dimension), and Thorium.

New Jersey   Clay, Greensand Marl, Peat, Sand and Gravel (construction and industrial), Stone (crushed), Titanium, and Zinc.

New Mexico   Cement (portland), Coal, Copper, Gold, Gypsum, Lead, Marble, Molybdenum, Natural Gas, Petroleum, Potash, Salt, Sand and Gravel (construction), Silver, Stone (crushed), Uranium, Vanadium, and Zinc.

New York Cement (portland), Clay, Emery, Garnet, Gypsum, Iron Ore, Lead, Limestone, Natural Gas, Petroleum, Salt, Sand and Gravel (construction), Sandstone, Silver, Slate, Stone (crushed), Talc, Titanium, Wollastonite, Peat, Marble, Gemstones, Mercury, and Zinc.

North Carolina Asbestos, Clay, Copper, Gold, Granite, Lithium, Marble, Mica, Phosphates, Sand and Gravel (construction and industrial), Stone (crushed), Talc, and Tungsten.

North Dakota Clay, Gemstones, Lignite, Lime, Natural Gas, Petroleum, Salt, Sand and Gravel (construction & industrial), and Uranium.

Ohio Cement(portland), Clay, Coal, Gypsum, Limestone, Natural Gas, Petroleum, Salt, Sand and Gravel (construction), Sandstone, and Stone (crushed).

Oklahoma Cement (portland), Coal, Gypsum, Helium, Lead, Limestone, Natural Gas, Petroleum, Sand and Gravel (construction and industrial), Stone (crushed), and Zinc.

Oregon Cement (portland), Diatomite, Gold, Lime, Mercury, Sand and Gravel (construction), Silver, Stone (crushed), and Uranium.

Pennsylvania Cement (masonry and portland), Clay, Coal, Cobalt, Iron Ore, Limestone, Natural Gas, Petroleum, Sand and Gravel (construction), Sandstone, Slate, Stone (crushed), and Zinc.

Rhode Island Gemstones, Sand and Gravel (construction and industrial), and Stone (crushed).

South Carolina Cement (masonry and portland), Clay, Mica, Sand and Gravel (construction & industrial), and Stone (crushed).

South Dakota Beryl, Cement (portland), Gold, Granite, Mica, Petroleum, Silver, Stone (crushed and dimension), Uranium, and Vanadium.

Tennessee Cement (portland), Clay, Coal, Copper, Iron Ore, Limestone, Marble, Phosphates, Pyrites, Sand and Gravel (construction), Sandstone, Stone (crushed), and Zinc.

Texas Cement (portland), Clay, Granite, Graphite, Gypsum, Helium, Iron Ore, Limestone, Magnesium Metal, Natural Gas, Petroleum, Salt, Sand and Gravel (construction), Silver, Stone (crushed), Sulfur, Talc, and Uranium.

Utah Beryllium, Clay, Coal, Copper, Gallium, Germanium, Gold, Gypsum, Iron Ore, Magnesium, Molybdenum, Natural Gas, Petroleum, Phosphates, Potash, Salt, Sand and Gravel (construction), Silver, Uranium, and Vanadium.

Vermont Asbestos, Granite, Marble, Sand and Gravel (construction), Slate, Stone (crushed and dimension), and Talc.

Virginia Cement (portland), Clay, Coal, Gypsum, Lead, Limestone, and Sand and Gravel (construction), Slate, Soapstone, Stone (crushed), Titanium, and Zinc.

Washington Cement (portland), Clay, Coal, Copper, Gold, Gypsum, Lead, Magnesium, Marble, Sand and Gravel (construction), Silver, Stone (crushed), Talc, Tungsten, Uranium, and Zinc.

West Virginia Cement (portland), Clay, Coal, Limestone, Natural Gas, Petroleum, Salt, Sand and Gravel (construction), and Stone (crushed).

Wisconsin Copper, Iron Ore, Lead, Limestone, Sand and Gravel (construction and industrial), Stone (crushed), and Zinc.

Wyoming Cement (portland), Clay, Coal, Diamonds, Helium, Iron Ore, Natural Gas, Petroleum, Phosphate, Soda Ash, Stone (crushed), Uranium, and Vanadium.

(Source: Minerals Information Institute)

acid   Liquid that is sour to taste, can eat away metals, and is neutralized by alkalis and bases; acids have a pH below 7.

acidic rock   A type of igneous rock that consists predominantly of light-colored minerals and more than two-thirds silica.

adit   A horizontal tunnel drilled into rock.

agglomerate   A rock made from the compacted particles thrown out by a volcano.

alkali   A liquid with a pH above 7; alkalis feel soapy and slimy.

alkaline rock   A type of igneous rock containing less than half silica and normally dominated by dark-colored minerals.

alloy   A metal that is made by combining two or more metals.

atomic number   The number of protons in the nucleus of an element's atom.

atomic weight   The average weight of the isotopes of an element.

augite   A dark green-colored silicate mineral containing calcium, sodium, iron, aluminum, and magnesium.

basalt   Basic fine-grained igneous volcanic rock; lava often contains vesicles.

basic rock   An igneous rock with silica content of less than two-thirds and containing a high percentage of dark-colored minerals.

batholith   A very large body of plutonic rock that was intruded deep into the Earth's crust and is now exposed by erosion.

bauxite   A surface material that contains a high percentage of aluminum silicate; the principal ore of aluminum.

carat   The unit of weight for gems; 1 carat equals 0.2 grams (0.007 ounces), or 200 milligrams.

carbonate minerals   Minerals formed with carbonate ions (e.g., calcite).

clarity   A measure of how clear and free of flaws a gemstone is.

cleavage   The tendency of some minerals to break along one or more smooth surfaces.

coal The carbon-rich, solid mineral derived from fossilized plant remains; found in sedimentary rocks; types of coal include bituminous, brown, lignite, and anthracite; a fossil fuel.

compound Substance that contains two or more different elements joined together by chemical bonds.

crystal A mineral that has a regular geometric shape and is bounded by smooth, flat faces.

crystal system A group of crystals with the same arrangement of axes.

crystalline A mineral that has solidified but been unable to produce well-formed crystals; quartz and halite are commonly found as crystalline masses.

crystallization The formation of crystals.

density Amount (or mass) of a substance in a certain volume; density is measured in grams per cubic centimeter or pounds per cubic foot.

ductile Can be stretched or drawn into a thin wire without breaking.

element A fundamental chemical building block; a substance that cannot be separated into simpler substances by any chemical means; oxygen and sulfur are examples of elements.

erosion The wearing away of a landscape.

facet One of the small, flat polished surfaces on a cut gem; to cut or grind facets on a gemstone.

feldspar The most common silicate mineral; it consists of two forms, plagioclase and orthoclase.

ferromagnesian mineral Dark-colored minerals such as augite and hornblende that contain relatively high proportions of iron and magnesium and low proportions of silica.

fossil fuel Any fuel that was formed in the geologic past from the remains of living organisms; the main fossil fuels are coal and petroleum (oil and natural gas).

fracture   To break unevenly, usually a characteristic of a mineral without cleavage.

gangue   The unwanted mineral matter found in association with a metal.

gem   A mineral, usually in crystal form, that is regarded as having particular beauty and value.

gemologist   A person who has successfully completed recognized courses in gemology (the science and study of gemstones) and has proven skills in identifying and evaluating gem materials.

geode   A hollow lump of rock (nodule) that often contains crystals.

granite   An acidic, igneous plutonic rock containing free quartz, typically light in color; plutonic equivalent of rhyolite.

group   The elements that make up one or more vertical columns in the periodic table.

gypsum   A mineral made of calcium sulfate.

halide minerals   A group of minerals (e.g., halite) that contain a halogen element (elements similar to chlorine) bonded with another element; many are evaporite minerals.

halite   A mineral made of sodium chloride.

igneous rock   Rock formed by the solidification of magma; igneous rocks include volcanic and plutonic rocks.

impermeable   A rock that will not allow a liquid to pass through it.

impurities   Small amounts of elements or compounds in an otherwise homogeneous mineral.

inert   The inability to combine with other elements or compounds.

ingot   A piece of pure metal, such as gold, made by pouring molten metal into a mold.

intrusive rock, intrusion   Rocks that have formed from cooling magma below the surface; when inserted among other rocks, intruded rocks are called an intrusion.

ion   A charged particle.

lapidary   A cutter, polisher, or engraver of precious stones.

luster   The way in which a mineral reflects light; used as a test when identifying minerals.

magma   The molten material that comes from the mantle and that cools to form igneous rocks.

malleable   Able to be hammered into shape without breaking.

metal   Any element in the periodic table that is shiny and that conducts electricity and heat well; most metals are also hard.

metalloid   An element that has some of the properties of a metal and some of the properties of a nonmetal.

micas   A group of soft, sheetlike silicate minerals (e.g., biotite, muscovite).

mineral   A naturally occurring inorganic substance of definite chemical composition (e.g., calcite, calcium carbonate).

mineral environment   The place where a mineral or a group of associated minerals forms; mineral environments include igneous, sedimentary, and metamorphic rocks.

mineralization   The formation of minerals within a rock.

mineralogist   A person who studies the formation, occurrence, properties, composition, and classification of minerals.

mineraloid   A substance that satisfies most, but not all, of the conditions of mineral classification (usually is not crystalline).

mixture   A substance made up of two or more elements or compounds that are not joined together by chemical bonds.

Mohs' scale   A relative scale developed to categorize minerals by hardness; the hardest is 10 (diamond), and the softest is 1 (talc).

native metal   A metal that occurs uncombined with any other element.

nonmetal   Any element in the periodic table that is not a metal or metalloid; most nonmetals are gases.

opaque   Allows no light through; not transparent or translucent.

open-pit mine   A mine with an open top, instead of tunnels under the Earth's surface.

ore   A rock containing enough useful metal or fuel to be worth mining.

ore mineral   A mineral that occurs in sufficient quantity to be mined for its metal; the compound must also be easy to process.

outcrop   The exposure of a rock at the surface of the Earth.

overburden   The unwanted layer(s) of rock above an ore or coal body.

oxide minerals   A group of minerals in which oxygen is a major constituent; a compound in which oxygen is bonded to another element or group.

oxidize   To combine with oxygen.

paleomagnetism   The natural magnetic traces that reveal the intensity and direction of the Earth's magnetic field in the geologic past.

period   A horizontal row in the periodic table.

permeable rock   A rock that will allow a fluid to pass through it.

placer deposit   A sediment containing heavy metal grains (e.g., gold) that have weathered out of the bedrock and have concentrated on a streambed or along a coast.

pyrite   Iron sulfide; it is common in sedimentary rocks that were poor in oxygen; it sometimes forms fossil casts.

quarry   A place where stone is dug up.

radioactivity   The process during which a substance gives off, or radiates, atomic particles.

reactive   Taking part in chemical reactions easily.

reactivity series   A list of common metals arranged in order of how quickly they react with other substances; the most reactive metals are at the top of the list.

reservoir rock   A permeable rock in which petroleum accumulates.

rock   A naturally occurring solid material containing one or more minerals.

rock cycle   The continuous sequence of events that causes mountains to be formed and then eroded before being formed again.

sandstone   A sedimentary rock composed of cemented sand-sized grains 0.06 to 2 mm in diameter.

schist   A metamorphic rock characterized by a shiny surface of mica crystals all oriented in the same direction.

semiconductor   A material with an electrical conductance halfway between conductors and nonconductors.

shaft   A vertical tunnel that provides access or ventilation to a mine.

shale   A fine-grained sedimentary rock made of clay minerals with particle sizes smaller than 2 microns.

slate   A low-grade metamorphic rock produced by pressure, in which the clay minerals have arranged themselves parallel to one another.

smelting   The process of melting a rock or mineral in order to extract or purify metal.

streak   The color of the powder of a mineral produced by rubbing the mineral against a piece of unglazed, white porcelain; used as a test when identifying minerals.

sulfides   A group of important ore minerals (e.g., pyrite, galena, and sphalerite) in which sulfur combines with one or more metals.

tarnish   To gradually become dull or discolored when exposed to air; the original shine and color can usually be restored with polishing.

translucent   Quality of an object in which some light passes through but the object cannot be clearly seen.

transparent   Clear; allows light to pass through so that you can see through it.

twinning   Two or more crystals of the same mineral growing together in a symmetrical way.

vitreous   Having a glassy luster.

Arem, Joel. *Color Encyclopedia of Gemstones.* 2nd ed. New York: Van Nostrand Reinhold, 1987.

Bains, Rae. *Rocks and Minerals.* Mahwah, N.J.: Troll Associates, 1985.

Bingham, Caroline. *Rocks and Minerals.* New York: DK Publishing, 2004.

Cipriani, Curzio, and Alessandro Boreli. *Gems and Precious Stones.* New York: Simon & Schuster, 1986.

Fuller, Sue. *Rocks and Minerals.* New York: Dorling Kindersley, 1995.

Gallant, Roy A. *Minerals.* Tarrytown, N.Y.: Marshall Cavendish Corporation, 2001.

Holden, Martin. *The Encyclopedia of Gemstones and Minerals.* New York: Facts On File, 1991.

Hurlbut, Cornelius S. Jr., and Robert C. Kammerling. *Gemology.* 2nd ed. New York: John Wiley & Sons, 1991.

Levi, Primo. *The Periodic Table.* New York: Random House, 1996.

McConnell, Anita. *The World Beneath Us.* New York: Facts On File, 1985.

Miller, Ron. *The Elements: What You Really Want to Know.* Minneapolis, Minn.: Twenty-First Century Books, 2006.

Moody, Richard. *The Concise Illustrated Book of Rocks and Minerals.* New York: W.H. Smith Publishers, 1990.

Oxlade, Chris. *Elements and Compounds.* Chicago, Ill.: Reed Educational & Professional Publishing, 2002.

Oxlade, Chris. *Metals.* Chicago, Ill.: Reed Educational & Professional Publishing, 2002.

Parker, Steve. *Rocks and Minerals.* New York: DK Publishing, 1992.

Quinn, Susan. *Marie Curie: A Life.* New York: Simon & Schuster, 1995.

Schumann, Walter. *Handbook of Rocks, Minerals, and Gemstones.* Boston, Mass.: Houghton Mifflin, 1993.

Sofiandes, Anna S., and George E. Harlow. *Gems & Crystals From the American Museum of Natural History: An Illustrated Guide to the History, Lore, and Properties of the Gems and Minerals of One of the World's Greatest Collections.* New York: Simon & Schuster, 1990.

Strathem, Paul. *Mendeleyev's Dream: The Quest for the Elements.* New York: St. Martin's, 2001.

Stwertka, Albert. *A Guide to the Elements.* New York: Oxford University Press, 2002.

INDEX

JULIE KERR CASPER holds B.S., M.S., and Ph.D. degrees in earth science with an emphasis on natural resource conservation. She has worked for the United States Bureau of Land Management (BLM) for nearly 30 years and is primarily focused on practical issues concerning the promotion of a healthier, better-managed environment for both the short- and long-term. She has also had extensive experience teaching middle school and high school students over the past 20 years. She has taught classes, instructed workshops, given presentations, and led field trips and science application exercises. She is the author of several award-winning novels, articles, and stories.